Amy Bizzarri

T0349158

111 Places
in Chicago
That You
Must Not Miss

Photographs by Susie Inverso

emons:

Bibliographical information of the Deutsche Nationalbibliothek
The Deutsche Nationalbibliothek lists this publication in
the Deutsche Nationalbibliografie; detailed bibliographical data
are available on the internet at http://dnb.d-nb.de.

© Emons Verlag GmbH
Cäcilienstraße 48, 50667 Köln
info@emons-verlag.de
All rights reserved
© Photographs: Susie Inverso, Crimson Cat Studios, except see page 239
Design: Eva Kraskes, based on a design
by Lübbeke | Naumann | Thoben
Maps: altancicek.design, www.altancicek.de
Printing and binding: Grafisches Centrum Cuno, Calbe
Printed in Germany 2025
ISBN 978-3-7408-2402-0
Revised new edition, February 2025

Guidebooks for Locals & Experienced Travellers
Join us in uncovering new places around the world at
www.111places.com

Foreword

Flying into Chicago at night over the vast, dark blue Lake Michigan, stars twinkling above, I hear Liz Phair's "Stratford-on-Guy" musings on returning home. From above, Chicago is peaceful, "lit from within," with its grid glowing amber. Covered with a blanket of freshly fallen snow, it's simply magical.

Chicago's seasons give us an edge. Long, cold winters make us strong. You can't call yourself a true Chicagoan until you've shoveled your car out of an alley packed with snow. Spring fills us up with flowers. They don't call us *Urbs in Horto* – City in a Garden – for nothing. Come summertime, we cherish our lakefront, chill over beer and BBQ, and cheer on the Cubs, our lovable losers. We don't give up. On anyone. Fall sees our trees dressed up in fiery red hues that recall the Great Fire of October 1871. This is a city that excels at rising from the ashes.

Here are the 111 off-the-radar places that conjure up the hard-working, inventive soul of Chicago: from the venues where music lifts us, including a mom-and-son-owned blues lounge and a thirties-era piano lounge hidden in an apartment building, to the places where we gather to place bets on racing turtles, fill our bellies with Chicago-style hot dogs, or welcome the full moon with a jam session on the beach. If you're looking for a little dose of Chicago's magic, snorkel the South Side limestone shelf that teems with life, or sip champagne from the clandestine cupola atop a Beaux Arts skyscraper. Every place highlights Chicago's ability to transform, rapidly and creatively: potholes morph into mosaics; vacant lots into apiaries; and industrial wastelands into serene spaces where wild creatures come to play.

Walking through the city that Sarah Bernhardt once christened "the pulse of America," I am reminded that it is Chicago's no-nonsense, broad-shouldered citizens who make it feel like home.

Welcome to my Windy City.

Amy Bizzarri

111 Places

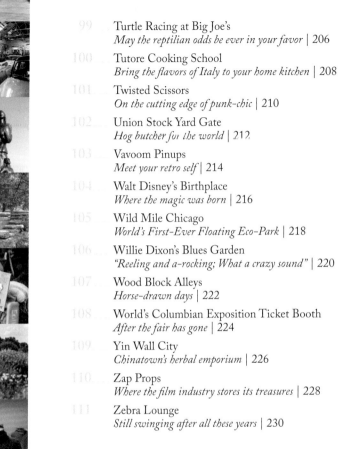

1 3 Arts Club Courtyard
A room of her own

In its almost 100-year history, the 3 Arts Club of Chicago served as a safe, supportive, and economical residence for over 13,000 young women as they studied the "three arts": music, painting, and drama. Founded in 1912 by social work pioneer Jane Addams and 30 other women from some of Chicago's wealthiest families, including social activist Edith Rockefeller McCormick, the club financed this beautiful, Byzantine building on swanky Dearborn Street with the goal of providing each resident, all promising young, female artists, with a room of her own as well as a chance to meet and collaborate with other artists in the same circumstances, all new to the city and working to find their way in the world of the arts.

Designed by Holabird and Roche, the building opened its arched main doors in 1914, and was complete with all the trappings of an artist's retreat within the big city: a library, tearoom, studio space, dining room, and three floors of dormitory rooms centered on a spacious, inspiring open courtyard.

The club provided the young women living there with both independence and security. The last residents moved out in 2004, and the building stood closed and unused until 2015, when Restoration Hardware moved into the 70,000-square-foot landmark build, and transformed it into a six-floor spectacle of a furniture store that feels like a museum. The grand staircase that once ushered up-and-coming artists out onto the town, a rooftop conservatory with stunning views of the Gold Coast, and a historic stage glittering with gilded mirrors – all were lovingly restored back to life after being shuttered for years.

The crown jewel is the courtyard, open year-round thanks to a new pyramid of glass and steel, with the grandest chandelier in the city of Chicago dripping from the pyramidion. Settle in for a northern-California-inspired menu and you'll be bathed in sunshine and surrounded by flowers, olive trees, and topiaries.

Address 1300 N Dearborn Parkway, Chicago, IL 60610, +1 (312) 475-9116 | Getting there Train to Clark/Division (Red Line) | Hours Mon–Fri 11:30am–8pm, Sat 10am–8pm, Sun 10am–7pm | Tip There is usually a wait for a table in the courtyard, so make the most of it by ordering a Bellini or a flute of fine champagne from the rear espresso counter, and head to the rooftop garden, where you can sip while enjoying the gorgeous views.

2 150 North Riverside

The champagne flute

Chicago has long been a laboratory for architectural innovation, and our city's skyline is a testament to creativity. Pioneers like William LeBaron Jenney (1832–1907) and Daniel Burnham (1846–1912) explored steel-frame construction and large areas of plate glass, creating the first modern skyscrapers. Later, architects like Louis Sullivan (1856–1924) emphasized verticality, while Ludwig Mies van der Rohe's (1886–1969) work at the Illinois Institute of Technology influenced supertall composite buildings worldwide.

Innovative architecture continues to rise towards the blue skies over Chicago. One recent building stands as a champagne-flute-shaped testament to Chicago-style ingenuity for defying structural norms and pushing the boundaries of architectural possibility. 150 North Riverside was completed in 2017, and it was the 2019 winner of the American Institute of Architects' highest award for design excellence.

For nearly 80 years, the 2-acre site where 150 North Riverside now stands was considered too troublesomely narrow for construction. Architects from Goettsch Partners and engineers from Magnusson Klemencic Associates (MKA) took on the challenge, squeezing a nearly 1.5 million-square-foot building onto the compact site. The result? A gravity-defying skyscraper that defies typical structural logic.

Unlike most tall buildings, this one is narrower at the bottom and widens at the upper floors. Caissons were drilled more than 110 feet below ground level into bedrock to provide a stable foundation in Chicago's swampy soil. The building's support system, the longest hot-rolled steel beams ever made in the US, allows the width of the 54-story tower to splay out from a mere 39 feet at the bottom to a spacious 120 feet at the top. Remarkably, the mega-columns on the north and south sides could support the weight of 26 fully loaded and fully fueled 747 jets.

Address 150 N Riverside Place, Chicago, IL 60606, +1 (312) 300-4462, www.150northriverside.com | Getting there Train to Clinton (Green Line) | Hours Unrestricted from the outside | Tip Nearby, eco-conscious River Point Park was built directly atop active Amtrak rail lines. Sound walls at its north and south ends help deaden train noise. The park also uses a rainwater-harvesting system to direct rainwater into storage tanks, where it is then used to irrigate the park's native plants (150 North Riverside Plaza, www.chicagoriverpoint.com).

3 The 606
Chicago's elevated escape

The 606, a 2.7-mile trail that connects four ground-level parks and four amazing Chicago neighborhoods, is set high above the city streets, on tall, steel-reinforced concrete embankments that once carried train tracks. Running eastward along Bloomingdale Avenue, from Ashland Avenue towards Ridgeway Avenue to the west, this glorious stretch of green space offers a bird's-eye view into Chicago city life.

The elevated Bloomingdale Line was built in 1915 to prevent freight trains from killing pedestrians at street-level crossings. Thirty-eight viaducts, still in place today, allowed passersby to make their way safely beneath the rails. In time, trucks began to replace trains, and the last freight cars made their way down from the line in 2001. Weeds took over the tracks, and the elevated line was closed to the public.

In the early 2000s, a grassroots organization dreamed up a plan for the neglected rail line. Smooth, wide pavement replaced the rails; colorful native prairie flowers replaced weeds. Runners, walkers, bikers, and nature lovers of all ages replaced trains. Today, kids learn to ride bicycles here; commuters use the trail as a shortcut to work; lovers walk into the sunset together. Vibrant art installations and dynamic, creative programming make each visit to the 606 different from the last.

The elevated 606 is an escape from the city that intersects the city, a place to catch your breath and see Chicago from a new perspective. Since it stands almost 20 feet above the streets, one can peer into the many windows that line the trail and look out over the city of Chicago, with a clear, sweeping view of its skyscraping skyline in the distance. The new trailway was named in honor of the zip code prefix – 606 – for the diverse neighborhoods that are now connected, not only by the three digits but also by this remarkable urban oasis.

Address Bloomingdale Avenue, from Ashland Avenue on the east to Ridgeway Avenue on the west, www.the606.org | Getting there There are 12 access points to the 606; visit the website for addresses and an interactive map | Hours Daily dawn–dusk | Tip Though you can always walk the length of the trail, renting a Divvy bike is the easy and fun way to explore the 606. There are 17 Divvy bike rental stations located within a block of the 606. Your best bet is to enter the trail at the Julia de Burgos Park access point, where you'll also find a Divvy station (1805 N Albany Avenue, www.divvybikes.com).

4 __ Alcala's Western Wear

Urban cowboy

Luis Alcala's story embodies Chicago's resilient spirit. Born in Durango, Mexico, Alcala's American Dream began unfolding when he immigrated to the United States, where he would find work picking cotton in the deep South before making his way to Chicago. This is where he and his wife Carmen raised a large family on the Northwest Side. He worked as a janitor and factory worker before setting up a table on Maxwell Street, where he hawked everything from men's belts to brooms.

In the early 1970s, he opened his brick-and-mortar Alcala's Men's Store, where he sold working men's wear and polyester suits à la *Saturday Night Fever* on the Southeast Side. But when nearby US Steel closed, taking away his clientele in turn, he opened a new store at 1733 W. Chicago Avenue. When the "Urban Cowboy" craze hit Chicago's streets, Alcala's sons convinced him to shift his focus. Before long, cowboy shirts, hats, belts, and boots were flying off the shelves.

It's impossible to miss the store today, a beacon of the Wild West on Chicago Avenue, with its iconic, life-sized, fiberglass horse greeting customers at the entrance. Alcala's, the largest Western-wear retailer in the Midwest, is famous for its fitted hats made from a variety of materials that include leather, straw, wool, and even chinchilla fur. Their ten-gallon cowboy hats command attention, and their silver and gold belt buckles shine with confidence. The boot collection ranges from affordable options in leather to luxurious alligator. Children can try on the coolest cow-kid duds in town and ride off into the sunset atop a vintage mechanical pony for a quarter.

The staff treat customers like family, and indeed, the Alcala family still runs the shop. Perks like free alterations and custom hat-shaping have made the store a cherished destination for Western wear enthusiasts from across the city and beyond.

Address 1733 W Chicago Avenue, Chicago, IL 60622, +1 (312) 226-0152,
www.alcalas.com | Getting there Train to Chicago or Division (Blue Line), or to Damen
or Ashland (Green Line) | Hours Mon–Thu 9:30am–6pm, Fri & Sat 9:30am–7pm,
Sun 9:30am–5pm | Tip Across the street, Forbidden Root (1746 W Chicago Avenue,
www.forbiddenroot.com/restaurants/restaurant-brewery), Chicago's first botanic brewery,
brews garden-inspired craft beers, such as the jasmine-spiked Purple Pils and the
strawberry-basil Hefeweizen.

5   Al Capone's Booth

Rhapsody at the Green Mill

Even though he owned a speakeasy in the basement across the street, gangster extraordinaire Al Capone loved the Green Mill Cocktail Lounge above all. When Scarface entered, the bandleader knew it was best to pause everything and play "Rhapsody in Blue" – pronto! From his favorite moss green, velvet-lined booth, directly across from the side-door entrance on Lawrence, near the end of the bar, Chicago's Big Fellow, as his criminal associates called him, could assess whoever entered the bar while simultaneously soaking in whatever act was onstage.

Capone's favorite crooner in the twenties was Joe E. Lewis. In 1927, Lewis was "asked" to sign a contract that required him to sing exclusively at the Green Mill, at the request of Jack "Machine Gun" McGurn, a mobster pal of Capone. When he refused, he was bludgeoned with a revolver, and his throat and tongue slashed with a hunting knife. Amazingly, he survived the attack and returned to perform as a comic at the Green Mill; McGurn went on to mastermind the Saint Valentine's Day Massacre. The Green Mill tells this story in part, on the large wood carving above the bar, which depicts the cast of characters and poetically sets the scene with the inscription: "Big Al was ingesting spaghetti / Machine Gun McGurn strangely still / Told Joe E., 'You'll look like confetti / If you try to quit the Green Mill.'"

If the walls of the Green Mill could talk, they'd have so many soulful stories to tell. From the jazz greats – Billie Holiday, Von Freeman, Wilbur Campbell, Kurt Elling, Orbert Davis – who mesmerized audiences in the once smoke-filled lounge, to the mobsters and movie stars who mingled over martinis in this timeless jazz bar, the Green Mill is haunted with legends of long ago. For over 100 years Ceres, Goddess of Harvest, has watched over the crowds in this Art Deco gem, the best jazz club in Chicago, and likely the world.

Address 4802 N Broadway, Chicago, IL 60640, +1 (773) 878-5552, www.greenmilljazz.com | Getting there Train to Lawrence (Red Line) | Hours Sun–Fri 4pm–1am, Sat 2pm–1am; see website for show schedule | Tip You can still catch great jazz at the Green Mill – as well as great poetry. Every Sunday night, 7pm–10pm, poets sling poems on the Green Mill's stage during the interactive Uptown Poetry Slam, the longest running slam in the city.

6 — Alfred Caldwell Lily Pool
Chicago's Prairie-style oasis

Tucked in a gated corner of Lincoln Park, the wild yet intimate Alfred Caldwell Lily Pool is easy to miss. It is a timeless, hidden oasis that promises a moment of peace in the middle of a city on the move.

Designed by renowned architect Alfred Caldwell, the pool's landscape recalls a lush, Illinois River valley dotted with wild flowers. Follow the stonework path that meanders along the lily-spotted lagoon, through the native-plant-filled landscape, and past the gurgling waterfall; ascend the stone steps to the circular council ring that overlooks the pond and offers a glimpse of Lake Michigan. This is perhaps the best spot in the city to relax and reflect.

Originally built in 1889 as an ornate, Victorian-style garden, the artificially-heated lily pool became home to frogs and invasive plants that soon undermined the intended, romantic feel. In 1936, Alfred Caldwell was hired by the Works Progress Administration to recover the overgrown, neglected garden. He strived to create a natural, Midwestern ecosystem contained within 2.7 acres in Lincoln Park. When the city park district cut the project budget, Caldwell was so set on his poetic plan that he cashed in his $5,000 life insurance policy for $250 and bought thousands of native plants from Sauk County, Wisconsin, planting them, together with his crew, the very next day. The result is an ode to the Midwest before the Europeans set foot on the river plains.

By the 1950s, migratory birds had claimed the gated getaway as a rookery of their very own, and the Lincoln Park Zoo followed their cue, transforming it into an avian exhibit. Before long, the birds and weeds took over, leading to further erosion. It wasn't until the Lincoln Park Conservancy stepped in that the landscape was restored to Caldwell's original vision, and the lily pool, a glorious example of Prairie-style landscape architecture, reopened in 2002.

Address 125 W Fullerton Parkway, Chicago, IL 60614, +1 (773) 883-7275, www.lincolnparkconservancy.org | **Getting there** CTA bus 151 to Stockton & Arlington or CTA bus 22 to Clark & Fullerton | **Hours** Daily 7:30am–7pm | **Tip** Built in the late 1890s to showcase exotic plants and flowers in a city that was rapidly industrializing, the nearby Lincoln Park Conservatory is an exotic-style Victorian-era glasshouse garden. A 50-foot-tall fiddle-leaf rubber tree, planted in 1891, still thrives in the lush Palm House (2391 N Stockton Drive, www.chicagoparkdistrict.com/parks).

7 — Athenian Candle
Tradition hand-dipped with love

Athenian Candle's beautiful lambathes, traditional Orthodox candles, have been the glowing light source for thousands upon thousands of weddings, baptisms, and religious holidays in Chicago's Near West Side Greek community for almost 100 years. Since it was founded in 1922, this family-owned cornerstone business has been making the cherished tapered candles in-house and with love.

Chicago's Greektown is centered on a bustling, four-block stretch of Halsted Street that runs from Madison to Van Buren. Themistocles Godelas, a candle maker in Greece, and his wife, Efthimia, founded Athenian Candle in 1922 on the corner of West Jackson, at the center of the Halsted action, not long after they immigrated to Chicago from Athens.

The lambathes at Athenian Candle are made of pure beeswax and recognized for their romantic, soft glow and smokeless, slow burn. Hand-dipped one paper-thin layer at a time, twelve to twenty-nine times, they come in sizes that vary from eight to sixty inches in height. These candles are central to Greek Orthodox ceremonies. For baptisms, children circle the font three times, carrying smaller lambathes. Brides and grooms each hold lighted candles during the traditional wedding ceremony.

In addition to their iconic lambathes, Athenian Candle carries oil lamps (*kandilia*), worry beads (*komboloi*) and wedding crowns (*stefana*). *Tamas*, small silver rectangles embossed with just about every ailing body part you can imagine, are ready to be whisked away to altars near and far as offerings for urgent health-related prayer requests.

Interestingly, the shop also carries a wide selection of spirit candles that promises to rid you of your money woes, find you a good husband or tame a terrible one, ban bad spirits from your home, and more. Ritualistic aerosol sprays will allegedly not only extinguish undesirable odors but also clear your psychic energy field.

Address 300 S Halsted Street, Chicago, IL 60661, +1 (312) 332-6988, www.atheniancandle.com | Getting there Train to UIC / Halsted (Blue Line) | Hours Mon–Tue & Fri 9:30am–6pm, Thu 9:30am–7pm, Sat 9:30am–5pm | Tip The National Hellenic Museum's Frank S. Kamberos Oral History Project is the largest national effort to record the Greek immigrant experience in America by interviewing and recording the life stories of Americans of Greek origin. Listen to the tales or record your own at the kiosk located in the permanent Greek Story in America exhibit (333 S Halsted Street, www.nationalhellenicmuseum.org).

8 Beautiful Rind

Savor the art of cheese

Cheese is "no less than a miracle," Chicago-based cheese monger Erika Kubick claims in her book, *Cheese Sex Death: A Bible for the Cheese Obsessed.* "It has the power to ground us in a connection to Mother Nature, the people who create blessings from Her gifts, and the history of civilization. There is something inextricably spiritual about cheese."

Beautiful Rind is a specialty cheese shop located in the charming, North Side neighborhood of Logan Square. Beyond its curated selection of high-quality cheeses from around the world, with an emphasis on those made in the Midwest, this full-service cheese shop offers a variety of charcuterie, an incredible selection of olives, nuts, and jams to complete your cheeseboard, and a carefully crafted, affordable wine selection, with many bottles priced at $20 or less.

"Cheesemakers take great care to nurture a rind that flavors and matures the milky alchemy lying just below the surface," explains owner Randall Felts. "To cheese mongers, the rind showcases the life of the cheese and all the love that went into its delicious creation. Rinds are alive, evolving, and they create the flavor that puts a blissful smile on all those who experience what's inside."

The streetside shop also offers lunch and dinner from a menu featuring enticing, cheese-centric dishes, like flaming bread cheese, grilled cheese sandwiches, classic French raclette, a tangy beer cheese served with freshly baked, Bavarian-style pretzels, and even a sundae made with three scoops of Blakesville chevre cheese topped with rosemary caramel sauce.

"Beautiful Rind is so modern, so chic, and its cheese mongers are so knowledgeable and friendly," writes Kubick. A dedicated in-shop classroom space hosts classes taught by staff mongers and cheese makers. Topics range from cheesy wine pairings to deep dives into cheddar's fascinating history.

Address 2211 N Milwaukee Avenue, Suite A, Chicago, IL 60647, +1 (312) 300-4535, www.beautifulrind.com | **Getting there** Train to California (Blue Line) | **Hours** Tue–Sun 11am–9pm | **Tip** Chicago's very own kitchen witch Jennifer Billock hosts workshops in Tyromancy, a form of divination that involves interpreting the patterns, shapes, and other characteristics of cheese to predict future events or gain insights into a person's fate (multiple locations including Beautiful Rind, www.kitchenwitch.substack.com/p/tyromancy-sessions).

9 Beer Baron Row

Brewing their fortunes

At the center of Chicago's eclectic Wicker Park neighborhood lies the eponymous triangular-shaped park that early developer Charles Wicker and his brother Joel donated to the city in 1870. After the Great Chicago Fire, the duo laid plans for a subdivision, with a mix of lot sizes, on their newly purchased 80 acres of land along Milwaukee Avenue. They made their fortune from homeless Chicagoans who had lost everything in the fire, and who were now looking westward to rebuild their houses and their lives.

Among Chicago's wealthy Northern European, beer-loving immigrants were the brewers themselves, who worked hard to rise from the ashes and reestablish their breweries. They made Wicker Park a neighborhood of their very own, building ornate Victorian mansions on the tree-lined streets, particularly Hoyne and Pierce Avenues, which became known as Beer Baron Row.

At 2137 W Pierce Avenue is the gingerbread-style mansion of German-American furniture tycoon Hermann Weinhardt. Across the street, the house at 2138 W Pierce Avenue, which once served as the Polish Consulate, features elaborate exterior Stick-Eastlake-style decorative wood carvings – the original owner was treasurer of a wood-milling company. Famed pianist Ignacy Paderewski once gave an outdoor concert from the veranda, and it has been known as the Paderewski House ever since. The Italianate dream of a mansion at 1407 N Hoyne Avenue is thought to be haunted: the original owner, German wine and beer merchant John H. Rapp, was murdered here by his bookkeeper.

1558 N Hoyne Street is one of the oldest homes in the area, having been built in 1877 for C. Hermann Plautz, founder of the Chicago Drug and Chemical Company. The metal exterior trim, a post-fire precaution, is worth noting. The real cannon displayed on the lawn remains from the years when the home served as an American Legion Hall.

Address N Hoyne Avenue and W Pierce Avenue, Chicago, IL 60622 | Getting there
Train to Damen (Blue Line) | Tip Many scenes from the 2000 hit movie *High Fidelity*
were filmed in buildings along Wicker Park's stretch of Milwaukee Avenue, including the
former Double Door venue (1572 N Milwaukee Avenue) and the fictional record store
Championship Vinyl (1500 N Milwaukee Avenue).

10 Beyond the Vines
Where diehard Cubs fans rest in peace

The Chicago Cubs, affectionately known as "the Lovable Losers" for a very long time, seemed destined to remain Major League Baseball's underdogs for all eternity. Though the team won back-to-back World Series championships in 1907 and 1908, and appeared in seven World Series following their 1908 title, most recently in 1945, their 108-year-long losing streak seemed unbreakable. But the strong fan base never gave up on their beloved Cubbies, and in 2016, when the Chicago Cubs beat out the Cleveland Indians to clinch the World Series title, after a century-long-plus wait, long-suffering Cubs fans wept tears of joy, burst into cheers and swarmed into the streets surrounding Wrigley Field. Once you're a Cubs fan, you're a Cubs fan forever.

At Bohemian National Cemetery, the most vehement Cubs fans can celebrate their beloved team's most recent victory and all future ones, even in the afterlife. The cemetery's "Beyond the Vines" Columbarium offers deceased Cubs fans the chance to be buried in an urn set inside a 24-foot-high brick wall covered with ivy, just like the famous and beloved ivy-covered outfield wall at Chicago's Wrigley Field.

The Cubbie Columbarium was the brilliant idea of Dennis Mascari, who, after paying a visit to the cemetery, decided that there had to be a better, happier backdrop beyond boring old gravestones for fans of the baseball club. The wall may seem a little creepy, but not to Cubs fans. Mascari himself was interred in one of its "Eternal Skyboxes" in 2011.

A stained glass scoreboard, a small patch of Wrigley turf and a bench reportedly used in the Cubs bullpen all provide the deceased yet die-hard fans who are buried here with the chance to spend eternity with the field that brought them so much joy during their lifetimes. Ballpark seats invite visitors to remember happier times, watching games unfold with their lost loved ones.

Address Bohemian National Cemetery, 5255 N Pulaski Road, Chicago, IL 60630, +1 (773) 539-8442, www.friendsofbnc.org | **Getting there** Train to Irving Park (Blue Line), then CTA bus 53 to Pulaski & Foster | **Hours** Daily 7:30am–5pm | **Tip** Chicago Mayor Anton Cermak, who was assassinated in 1933 when he took a bullet intended for President Franklin Roosevelt, is buried in an Art Deco-style mausoleum at Bohemian National Cemetery. Inscribed on the marble enclosing the tomb are the famous last words Cermak spoke to Roosevelt: "I'm glad it was me instead of you."

11 Brunk Children's Museum of Immigration

Welcome, step aboard a steamship to America

Would you leave home today in search of a better tomorrow? Imagine saying goodbye to the life you know, sailing away in steerage on a steamship, and setting foot onto a new, promised land, where a new language, culture, and plenty of hard work await. The Brunk Children's Museum of Immigration bridges past and present, giving children a small taste of the challenging lives of the immigrants that built Chicago.

It is hard to believe that at one time there were more Swedes in Chicago than in any city outside of Stockholm. In the late 1800s, the Swedish-born population in Chicago increased by roughly 233 percent, and by 1930 there were 65,735 Swedish-born Chicagoans and more than 140,000 children of Swedish immigrants settled in Chicago. Most settled in the North Side neighborhood of Andersonville, the heart of which is considered the corner of Clark Street and Berwyn Avenue, where you'll find the Brunk Children's Museum of Immigration housed within the Swedish American Museum.

Kids at this strictly hands-on museum enter Old World Sweden first, where a traditional Scandinavian red stuga house and many farm chores await. Then it's time to pack their belongings in a trunk and make the move to the New World, via the replica 20-foot steamship. Upon arrival in America, kids can settle into a pioneer log cabin and get to work milking the cow, farming a small plot of land, setting the table for dinner, bringing in firewood and more.

Be sure to check out the Swedish American Museum's permanent exhibit, The Dream of America: Swedish Immigration to Chicago. Members of the Andersonville community shared precious family keepsakes, including passports, handcrafted heirlooms and steamship tickets to bring this community-sourced exhibit to life.

Address 5211 N Clark Street, Chicago, IL 60640, +1 (773) 728-8111, www.swedishamericanmuseum.org | Getting there Train to Berwyn (Red Line) | Hours Mon–Thu 1–4pm, Fri 10am–4pm, Sat & Sun 11am–4pm | Tip Simon's Tavern is Chicago's unofficial Swedish outpost, a dive bar with Viking decor and ship-like ambiance thanks to a bar modeled after a French steamship (5210 N Clark Street).

12   Bubbly Creek

Reclaiming nature from the Jungle

In the early 20th century, the pristine South Fork of the Chicago River morphed into an open sewer for the Union Stock Yards. Meatpackers dumped so much blood, entrails and offal into what was once a serene wetland that it began to bubble with methane and hydrogen sulfide gas; its banks were coated in animal hair and waste.

It was so polluted that in 1906, author Upton Sinclair wrote in The Jungle, his expose on Chicago's meatpacking industry, "… the filth stays there forever and a day … bubbles of carbonic gas will rise to the surface and burst, and make rings two or three feet wide …". The so-called Bubbly Creek was so caked with grease and filth that Sinclair observed runaway chickens walking upon the mucky fork. It wasn't until the Union Stock Yards closed in 1971 that Bubbly Creek began ever so slowly to reclaim its once pristine state.

The best way to explore Bubbly Creek is by kayak. From the newly inaugurated Park 571 Boathouse, you can launch a canoe or kayak directly into the northern starting point of the fork and easily paddle its length southward, to the end point at Pershing Road.

Paddling along the Bubbly Creek, it is incredible to see the animals and vegetation that are slowly reclaiming their wetland home. If you are lucky, you might spot mallard ducks navigating the waters, swooping tree swallows, elegant green herons, high-flying hawks or evidence of beavers busily building homes of their own along the banks. But the creek, despite efforts to help speed along the renewal process, still bears witness to its highly polluted past: rebar pokes out from the embankments, plastic bags decorate the trees that flank the creek, and bubbles still rise up from the turbid depths. Though Bubbly Creek still has a long way to go, considering its past, it is truly amazing that one can paddle it and find peace as well as signs of renewal and hope.

Address Park No. 571, 2754 S Eleanor Street, Chicago, IL 60608, +1 (312) 747-6515, www.chicagoparkdistrict.com/parks | Getting there Train to Ashland (Orange Line) | Hours Daily dawn–dusk | Tip Kayak Chicago (+1 (312) 852-9258, kayakchicago.com) offers private, guided kayak tours of Bubbly Creek. If you prefer bringing your own kayak and paddling independently, Park No. 571, the starting point of the South Fork, has a public access launching pier.

13 Bughouse Square

Chicago's premier free speech forum

If you have something to say, pick up your soapbox and head to Bughouse Square. The square is Chicago's most celebrated, improvised, free speech center, located across from the historic Newberry Library in stroll-worthy Washington Square Park. This orator-friendly square has been hosting poets, religionists, political activists, cranks, and anyone else who has something timely or trivial to get off their chest since the 1920s.

Once a cow path with a well for thirsty cattle, Washington Square Park was transformed during the late 1800s into the bucolic park it is today, with its diagonal walkways bisecting manicured greenery towards a central fountain. In the park's heyday during the Roaring Twenties, revolutionary leftists unofficially began setting up their soapboxes here and declaring their truths. Many of the square's soapbox public speakers became legendary, including radical Lucy Parsons, whom the Chicago Police Department described as "more dangerous than a thousand rioters," anarchist and self-declared hobo doctor Ben Reitman, and Marxist feminist Martha Biegler. The name the square came to be called – Bughouse – is indicative of the public's perception of the early speakers as outrageous, thought to be too far ahead of their times. (The term "bughouse" was slang at the time for a mental health facility.)

In 1964, Life magazine profiled the popular square, marking it as a meeting place for gay men and women. In June 1970, Chicago's first Gay Pride March set off proudly from the park towards the Civic Center.

Today a Bughouse Square Committee, headquartered at Newberry Library, still organizes an annual free-speech extravaganza, known as the Bughouse Square Debates, in conjunction with the library's annual book sale.

A memorial tablet at the west end of the park declares Bughouse Square "Chicago's Premier Free Speech Forum."

Address 901 N Clark Street, Chicago, IL 60610, www.chicagoparkdistrict.com/parks | Getting there Train to Chicago (Red Line) | Hours Unrestricted | Tip Free and open to the public, the Newberry Library, located on the northern edge of the square, is home to more than 1.5 million books, 5 million manuscript pages, and 500,000 historic maps. Request to view the 1692 fur trade contract in the museum's collection, which contains one of the earliest references to "Chicagou" (60 W Walton Street, www.newberry.org).

14 Busy Beaver Button Museum

Pin on a button and broadcast your message

The Busy Beaver Button Co. and Button Museum stands as the world's only pin-back button museum. Located within the company's small-scale manufacturing headquarters, this tiny museum displays 9,000 rare, historical buttons. There seems to be a button for every television show, movie, product, and even presidential candidate from past and present (including the "pre-button" made in support of Lincoln's 1864 presidential campaign), a WWII button that depicts Uncle Sam hanging Adolf Hitler from a tree, and an ultrarare Oswald the Lucky Rabbit button from 1929.

Wearing political buttons, a largely American tradition, began with the inauguration of George Washington in 1789. Supporters of our nation's first president wore "Washington Inaugurals," large, hand-stamped buttons made of copper, brass or Sheffield plate on their coats and breeches. Busy Beaver's "Long Live the President GW" brass button is the oldest and most valuable in the museum's collection.

Busy Beaver Button Co. started in owner Christen Carter's college apartment in the mid-nineties. Four million buttons later, the small company is the leader in the button industry, producing custom buttons made of metal, wood and even 24-karat gold. Every custom button is made with solar power from recycled steel in their geothermally heated/cooled headquarters in the hip Logan Square neighborhood. Busy Beaver's clients include individuals, large corporations, and cultural institutions, from the Brooklyn Brewery to the Art Institute of Chicago. The Busy Beaver Button Museum was unveiled within the production facility in 2010.

As you browse the museum, you can also see button manufacturing in action, as all of the company's buttons are produced onsite, largely by hand. You can even make a button of your very own upon request.

Address 3407 W Armitage Avenue, Chicago, IL 60647, +1 (773) 645-3359, www.busybeaver.net | Getting there Train to Belmont (Blue Line), then CTA bus 82 to Kimball & Armitage | Hours Mon–Fri 9am–5:30pm | Tip Discuss pin politics barside at Scofflaw, an elegant corner bar with a Victorian-meets-modern vibe, just a three-minute walk down Armitage Avenue from the Busy Beaver Button Museum. You'll find over 80 types of gin at the antique bar, as well as small plates and a fine selection of American craft beers on draught (3201 W Armitage Avenue, www.scofflawchicago.com).

15 Calumet Fisheries

Seafood shack beside the Blues Brothers' bridge

Who can forget the scene in the iconic 1980 John Landis film, when the Blues Brothers, "Joliet" Jake and Elwood Blues, jump their retired police cruiser over the open 95th Street bascule bridge? Calumet Fisheries, located just off that memorable, moveable bridge on the banks of the heavily industrialized Calumet River in South Deering, saw the scene unfold. This tiny little fish shack has been smoking up sable, salmon, sturgeon, and more marine delights than you can count on ten greasy fingers since the 1920s, long before the Blues Brothers cruised on by.

One of two smokehouses still allowed to burn wood and smoke its fish in the city, this family owned and operated South Side institution smokes all of its seafood on site, stoking the fire and flavor with oak logs, and never, ever using liquid smoke or other industrial substitutes. Before hitting the smoker, the fruits of the seas are marinated overnight. Many customers swear by the golden brown, sweet smoked chubs and salivate over the garlic pepper smoked salmon. Give the smelt – an unofficial Midwestern delicacy – a try too. These finger-sized fish were an invasive species that somehow escaped from Michigan's Crystal Lake into Lake Michigan in the early 1920s.

The smoked goods make up only half of the no-nonsense menu. The other half features fried fish, notably catfish, clam strips, frogs' legs, and shrimp. Sides are mostly deep-fat fried, too – think French fries, onion rings, breaded mushrooms, and pickle spears. A side cup of crackers costs just 55 cents.

Don't expect a fancy menu, seating or even bathrooms. This is strictly a take-out business. Do as most diners here do, and dig into your goods right away in the comfort of your car, parked out front. If you're lucky, the drawbridge might pop up – but don't expect another Blues Brothers' style high-jinx jump.

Address 3259 E 95th Street, Chicago, IL 60617, +1 (773) 933-9855, www.calumetfisheries.com | Getting there Train to South Chicago (93rd) (Metra Electric Line) | Hours Sun–Wed 10am–9:45pm, Thu 9am–9:30pm, Fri & Sat 9am–9:45pm | Tip Want to catch and smoke your own fish? River Park, located on the Chicago River at 5100 N Francisco Avenue, near Foster Avenue, is one of the best fishing spots in the city. You'll need an Illinois fishing license, which you can obtain online before you go at www.dnr.illinois.gov.

16 Calumet Water Reclamation Plant

Looking beyond the (toilet) bowl

One hundred and fifty years ago, city sewage dumped into the Chicago River or Lake Michigan, threatening the drinking water and the heath of early Chicagoans. Thanks to the ingenuity of engineers, our city was saved from a swampy, unsanitary fate. On a Calumet Water Retention Plant tour, you can see firsthand how Chicago revolutionized the water treatment arena, as you witness where everyone's poop travels beyond the bowl and what happens to the water that flows down your home's drains.

Organized as the Sanitary District of Chicago in 1889 under an act of the Illinois General Assembly District, the Metropolitan Water Reclamation District is credited with reversing the flow of the Chicago and Calumet River Systems. Today the district continues to protect Lake Michigan, the city's water source, and to guard businesses and homes against flood damage as it manages humanity's vital resource: water.

The District's seven modern water reclamation plants treat residential and industrial wastewater, while also guarding our lakes and rivers against hazardous substances and toxic chemicals. Each day, these hardworking plants clean and recover resources from wastewater as they pump more than 480 million gallons a day of raw sewage. The plant tour shows you all the action and the magnificent machinery, from the mechanical screens lifting rags and rocks from raw sewage, to the huge circular vats that separate sludge from liquid. You might pick up a few interesting scents along the tour, but this busy plant keeps Chicago safe and healthy while also blazing a new trail in the field of resource recovery. The plant is on the path to become energy neutral by 2050, while also recovering water, biosolids compost, algae for bioplastics, and phosphorus to be sold as fertilizer.

Address 400 E 130th Street, Chicago, IL 60628, +1 (312) 751-6635, www.mwrd.org | Getting there Train to 95th / Dan Ryan (Red Line), then CTA bus 34 to 130th Street & Daniel Drive | Hours Tours Tue 9am by reservation; group tours can be scheduled in advance | Tip You'll need to call +1 (312) 751-6633 or email tours@mwrd.org to reserve your plant tour. Anyone over 18 years of age must provide a scan or photocopy of their state ID or passport for a security check, and present it on the day of tour. For safety, wear long pants and sturdy shoes.

17 _ Chicago Bath House

Steam your cares away

If you're looking to steam out all the toxic elements from your life, or if you'd just love to indulge in a few vodka shots, borscht, and blini following a deep tissue massage, make a beeline to Chicago Bath House, a modern, Russian-style spa housed in a historic Chicago bathhouse.

Because of inadequate indoor plumbing in most homes, it wasn't until the early 1900s that Chicagoans began to bathe with regularity. Thanks to a push for public bathhouses, led by the Municipal Order League and three women physicians, city officials established 21 small and utilitarian public bathhouses in poor and immigrant neighborhoods between 1894 and 1918. One of these bathhouses was the Division Street Russian and Turkish Baths, which opened in 1906 and offered separate bathing facilities for men and women. In 2013, it was transformed into today's Chicago Bath House. Check out the original brick ovens in both the men's and women's *banya*, or hot rooms. If you can manage to open the door without burning your hands, you will spot giant granite boulders inside, which are heated to 800 degrees F every night with gas jets, maintaining their heat throughout the following day.

Give the traditional *platza* spa treatment a try. You will be lightly whipped with birch, eucalyptus, or oak branches by an esthetician as you lie flat on a wooden bench in the *banya*. Your eyes will be covered with a cool facecloth, so you will be even more surprised when the esthetician dumps icy cold water on your body. While it might not prove to be the most relaxing spa treatment you will ever experience, it will undoubtedly improve your circulation temporarily and open up your pores – both essentials if you are looking to detox.

Autographed photos of celebrity visitors line the first-floor hallway, and if you're lucky you might run into a famous person or two dressed to the nines in a bathrobe.

Address 1914 W Division Street, Chicago, IL 60622, +1 (773) 227-2284, www.bathhousechicago.com | **Getting there** Train to Division (Blue Line) | **Hours** Mon–Thu 10am–11pm, Fri 10am–noon, Sat 7am–noon, Sun 7am–11pm | **Tip** Chicago Bath House's first-floor restaurant and bar resembles an elegant, 19th-century luxury train dining car and features all your Russian favorites. While it's not necessarily low-calorie spa cuisine, you're welcome to dine in your waist-friendly spa robe.

18 — Chicago Fire Department Training Facility

Where Mrs. O'Leary's cow kicked over that lantern

"Late one night, when we were all in bed / Mrs. O'Leary lit a lantern in the shed / Her cow kicked it over, then winked her eye and said / 'There'll be a hot time in the old town tonight!'" (Chicago folk song). Mrs. Catherine O'Leary recalled hearing fiddle music as she got into bed on the night of Sunday, October 8, 1871. Hours later, she awoke to find her small barn at 137 DeKoven Street aflame. Flames whirled across the city. Two days later, more than 2,000 acres of Chicago had burned to the ground, over 300 lives were lost, and 100,000 were left homeless.

The Chicago Times jumped to the conclusion that O'Leary had burned down her barn herself. It described the 44-year-old mother of five as "an old Irish woman" who was "bent almost double with the weight of many years of toil, trouble and privation. … The old hag swore she would be revenged on a city that would deny her a bit of wood or a pound of bacon." Theories abound as to who or what caused the Great Chicago Fire, but fingers no longer point towards poor Mrs. O'Leary and her cow. In 1997, Chicago's city council officially exonerated the unlikely duo.

Today the Fire Department's Quinn Fire Academy stands on the very spot where the fire began. Step inside the lobby to see one of Chicago's original steam-powered engines, as well as a poignant display of the badges and bronzed boots and helmets of firefighters fallen in the line of duty. A 33-foot bronze sculpture of stylized flames entitled Pillar of Fire by sculptor Egon Weiner marks where Mrs. O'Leary's cow kicked over the lantern, just outside the academy. If you smell smoke while visiting the site of Mrs. O'Leary's barn, don't fret: as part of the cadets' training, instructors build live fires.

Address 558 W DeKoven Street, Chicago, IL 60607, +1 (312) 747-7239, www.cpfta.com | **Getting there** Train to Clinton (Blue Line) | **Hours** Mon–Fri 8:30am–3:30pm | **Tip** If you want to visit a real-life, former working Chicago firehouse, head to the Fire Museum of Greater Chicago, which is currently housed in what used to be Engine 123's quarters. Photographs, fire-fighting gear and equipment from throughout the ages and even old engines are all on display in this two-story firehouse. Currently the museum is only open on the fourth Saturday of each month, and closed entirely in December (5218 S Western Avenue, www.firemuseumofgreaterchicago.org).

19 Chicago Honey Co-op
Saving the honeybees, one hive at a time

If you spot a swarm of honeybees while you are strolling the streets of Chicago, you are not dreaming. The city is absolutely abuzz with bees thanks to Chicago Honey Co-op, a Lawndale-based organization that combines job training with the art of beekeeping. Since 2004, more than fifty beehives have buzzed with bees at their three urban apiaries. These city dwelling bees buzz around Humboldt, Garfield, and Douglas Parks, where a variety of flower and tree species coupled with diverse, highly concentrated nectars, make for an intensely flavored, all-natural, delicious honey. In addition to producing and selling raw honey, this sweet co-op teaches beekeeping, trains with hard-to-employ Chicagoans, and advocates sustainable agriculture.

If you want to see the Chicago Honey Co-op's bees in action, head to one of their three bee farms. Schulze & Burch Biscuit Company (1133 W 35th Street) in Bridgeport is home to about 20 hives, and the green rooftop of Christy Webber Landscaping (2900 W Ferdinand Street) hosts a handful of hives. Twelve hives are located in Back of the Yards near 51st and Racine, and two hives call Patchwork Farms (2825 W Chicago Avenue) home. If you're lucky, you might see beekeepers at work dressed in their light-hued suits and netted hats, checking each hive's "super" – vertical drawers where the bees store their honey. Puffs from the odd, teapot-shaped smoke machine help to calm the buzzing bees, while a large brush is used gently to brush the bees away from the supers, revealing the sweet, sticky treasure.

Chicago Honey Co-op is a community resource that produces more than just amber waves of certified natural honey. As the number of native bees is seeing sharp declines, this co-op passes the beekeeping torch to budding urban apiculturists while also fostering the community and saving the honeybees, one hive at a time.

Address 2000 W Carroll Avenue, Chicago, IL 60612, +1 (312) 508-8142, www.chicagohoneycoop.com | Getting there Train to Ashland (Green and Pink Line) | Hours See website for class and events schedule | Tip If you'd rather avoid the bees, you can also purchase Chicago Co-op Honey from the hive-free Green City Market, Chicago's only year-round, sustainable farmers' market. Located on the south end of Lincoln Park (1817 N Clark Street, www.greencitymarket.com) from May through October, this glorious, green market moves into the Peggy Notebaert Nature Museum (2430 N Cannon Drive, www.naturemuseum.org) from November through April.

20 Chicago Motor Club Inn
Trippy monument to motordom

The grand Chicago Motor Club building is Chicago's finest Art Deco-style skyscraper. When it formally opened on January 28, 1929, a Chicago Tribune reporter referred to it as "a monument to the progress of motordom." Originally designed by Chicago architectural firm Holabird and Root, in 2004 this 15-story skyscraper stood unoccupied and in danger of falling into complete disrepair. Thankfully, Hampton Inn stepped in, completely renovating the building and transforming it into a fabulous hotel that honors Chicago's original temple of transportation.

Founded by a group of automobile enthusiasts who shared an interest in both auto touring and racing, the Chicago Motor Club, which eventually merged into AAA, embraced road travel by providing maps, travel itineraries and hotel guides. The club offered visitors the chance to plan their new big trip thanks to TripTiks, maps that also provided tips on where to eat and stay along the highway, available in the lobby.

A 30-by-20-foot road map mural, painted by Chicago artist John Warner Norton, and still located above the elevators in the grand, two-story lobby, provided inspiration. Motor Club visitors studied the mural while dreaming up travel plans by following the grey lines, or the 19 national highways that existed in 1928, from Chicago to their desired, fantasy destination. An original, 1928 Ford Model A – the first Ford to use a standard set of driver controls including clutch and brake pedals, throttle, and gearshift – overlooks the lobby from the mezzanine.

"From the moment guests walk into the lobby, one immediately knows that this building is special," enthuses Ross Guthrie, the hotel's general manager. "The large mural of the map is stunning. We love telling the story of the building and sharing the integral part of history this building has had in Chicago and AAA."

Address 68 E Wacker Place, Chicago, IL 60601, +1 (312) 419-9014, www.hamptoninn3.hilton.com | Getting there Train to State/Lake (Brown, Orange, Purple, Green, and Pink Line) | Hours Unrestricted | Tip Try the "Giggle Water" (the code name for booze during Prohibition), a cocktail complete with gin, rum, tonic, simple syrup, lime, and parsley, with a splash of bourbon, at Jack's Place, the lobby bar.

21__Chicago Pizza & Oven Grinder Co.

Deep-dish pizza with a side of mob history

At 10:30am on February 14, 1929, four men packing two Thompson submachine guns burst into a garage at 2122 N Clark Street. They shot dead seven men of the North Side Irish gang associated with the Irish gangster George "Bugs" Moran, one of Al Capone's long-time enemies. Though the Saint Valentine's Day Massacre, as it came to be called, was never officially linked to Capone, most hold him responsible for the murders. And though the garage was demolished in 1967, you can still dig into a unique deep-dish pizza at the three-story brownstone building that likely served as a lookout, located just across the street.

Chicago Pizza & Oven Grinder Co. is best known for a one-of-a-kind take on Chicago-style deep-dish pizza that many refer to as an upside-down pizza in a bowl. "Made from scratch" with triple-raised Sicilian bread-type dough; a tangy homemade sauce brewed to perfection with olive oil, fresh garlic, onions, green peppers, whole plum tomatoes and a special blend of cheeses; sausage made from prime Boston butts; and whole, fresh mushrooms – pizzas here arrive tableside for eager diners to bite into. Oven Grinder Co. pizzas fall more within the pot pie classification: large, deep, and stuffed to the brim. They are baked in a crock, their dough puffed up several inches above the edge.

Rumor has it that the garage served as a lookout post for Capone's henchmen. Some 70 rounds of ammunition were fired on that fateful Valentine's Day, which many say marked the beginning of Capone's downfall. No one was brought to trial for the murders. Capone was subpoenaed, posted bond, and was released, only to be arrested in Philadelphia on charges of carrying concealed weapons. He served a mere nine months in prison before being released for good behavior.

Address 2121 N Clark Street, Chicago, IL 60614, +1 (773) 248-2570, www.chicagopizzaandovengrinder.com | Getting there Train to Sedgwick (Brown and Purple Line) | Hours Mon–Thu 4–10pm, Fri 4–11pm, Sat 11am–11pm, Sun 11am–10pm | Tip The Chicago History Museum's incredible virtual reality app Chicago 00: St. Valentine's Day Massacre offers a YouTube video and Google Street View experience, with images of the site of the massacre that can be viewed as high-resolution, 360° panoramas. Both experiences can be accessed online at www.chicago00.org.

22 — Chicago Underground Comedy

Sanctuary for the uncommon comedian

In a punk-rock setting on an infamous Tuesday nighttime slot, Chicago's hilarious comedians hit the stage of Lakeview's Beat Kitchen for Chicago Underground Comedy, or ChUC as it is best known, the second longest running and the most out-of-the-box and under-the radar comedy show in the city. Committed to weirdness, the lineups at this intimate show always include a sketch, character, and variety act, interspersing stand up with something spicy and different to cleanse the palette, as well as an act you couldn't even begin to classify. With tickets running at a whopping $5, ChUC stands as a laughably cheap date night. A percentage of ticket proceeds are dedicated to ChUC Charities, the show's in-house fundraising effort, which raises money for community-focused charities, giving you an even bigger bang for your buck.

Since 2005, ChUC has launched some of the most clever, innovative minds in the business, while also providing a sanctuary for comedians who just want to have fun and connect, and not necessarily do their tightest (or cleanest) ten minutes for the audience. Everyone has graced the small stage, from T. J. Miller to Cameron Esposito, Kyle Kinane to Hannibal Buress, Beth Stelling to Kumail Nanjiani. As an alt-comedy haven, ChUC revels in its reputation as a comics' playground. Silly goofs, wacky antics, and plain old tomfoolery are always welcome. This playground is also committed to inclusivity: women, people of color, and the LGBT community are reflected in the especially diverse lineups. Plan on trading a few laughs for tears, too, as the last Tuesday of the month is dedicated to Comedy Secrets, a secrets-and-sadness storytelling-based show.

The show starts at 9:30pm every Tuesday night at the Beat Kitchen and usually rocks a full house, so arrive early to save your seats.

Address Beat Kitchen, 2100 W Belmont Avenue, Chicago, IL 60618, www.chicagoundergroundcomedy.com, tours@mwrd.org | Getting there Train to Belmont (Red and Blue Line), then CTA bus 77 to Belmont & Hoyne | Hours Tours Tue 9am by reservation; group tours can be scheduled in advance | Tip Beat Kitchen serves up hearty pub grub during ChUC. Build your own pizza or dig into the spicy mac 'n' cheese while you enjoy the show. Save room for a homemade brownie (www.beatkitchen.com).

23   Chris's Billiards

The color of money

Chris's Billiards boasts, "It's not what's new, it's what's not new that's great." Not much has changed since legendary director Martin Scorsese stepped in this Portage Park gem and declared it the backdrop for the timeless pool-hall tale *The Color of Money*.

When production manager Dodie Foster arrived in Canada, where the movie was originally set to be filmed, he was disappointed to find mostly snooker tables. So he brought Scorsese to his hometown of Chicago and ushered him up the long staircase that leads to Chris's second-floor hall. The dozens of framed photographs of championship players on the walls made it obvious that this was a pool hall for professionals, and Scorsese cast Chris's as the hall where pool shark Fast Eddie Felson (played by Paul Newman in the movie) would groom Vincent Lauria (a young Tom Cruise) for pool stardom.

Chris's remains a place for players who are looking for low rates and good competition, making it an excellent place to learn the ropes of the game. Forty tables – ten seven-foot pool tables, twenty-nine nine-foot pool tables, and one twelve-foot snooker table – clack with both amateurs and pros. When you are not playing, settle into the bleachers and watch the tournaments go down. The competitions, with cash payouts of up to $5,000, have drawn the best pool players from around the world, including 1994 world champion Sang Lee, making Chris's a place where you can both learn and play beside or against the pros. As an added bonus, it is BYOB.

A musty smell lingers in the air, and pool sharks search high and low for their next meal ticket. The felt on the tables is worn. The stucco walls have taken in a lot of cigarette smoke over the years. But these are the telltale signs that Chris's is the real deal, with tables that play fast and zero room for restraint when it comes to the English you put on the cue ball.

Address 4637 N Milwaukee Avenue, Chicago, IL 60630, +1 (773) 286-4714, www.chrissbilliards.com | **Getting there** Train to Jefferson Park (Blue Line) | **Hours** Daily 9–2am | **Tip** Coffee shop by day and bar at night, Surge Coffee Bar & Billiards boasts 14 Brunswick Crown V pool tables and a modern, smoke-free, and friendly ambiance (3241 W Montrose Avenue, surgebilliards.com).

24 Civil War Memorial at St. James Cathedral

Faith over fire

At 9pm on October 8, 1871, a fire started in a small barn just south-west of Chicago's Loop. When flaming debris blew across the river, advancing the fire towards the ritzy Near North neighborhood of McCormickville, panic set in. The bells of St. James Cathedral rang close to midnight, warning the wealthy residents that their lives were in danger. More than 2,000 city acres had been flattened; 100,000 of Chicago's 300,000 inhabitants were left homeless. Only the stone walls, bell tower, and Civil War Memorial of St. James Cathedral, the oldest Episcopal Church in Chicago and a cornerstone of the neighborhood, had survived the fire.

When early settler Juliette Kinzie founded the parish here in 1834, this plot of land was surrounded by a vast wilderness. The city of Chicago was still but a dream. As the smoke began to clear that fateful fall, the weary yet faithful neighborhood parishioners built a temporary chapel on the site as soon as rubble had been cleared away. They gathered before the Civil War Memorial, which served as a makeshift altar, and held their first, poignant, post-fire mass.

The elaborate, mid-Victorian Civil War memorial was dedicated to parishioners who served during the bloodiest war in US history. Located today in the cathedral's narthex, the memorial features the names of seventy members who had enlisted in the Union Army; ten lost their lives. President elect Abraham Lincoln attended services at St. James on November 25, 1860. A plaque set in the north wall of the narthex honors his role in the Civil War.

Four years after the fire, on October 9, 1875, services were held in the rebuilt cathedral. At the top of the surviving bell tower, note the black stones, soot-stained from the Chicago Fire, a powerful reminder of the worst disaster in Chicago's history.

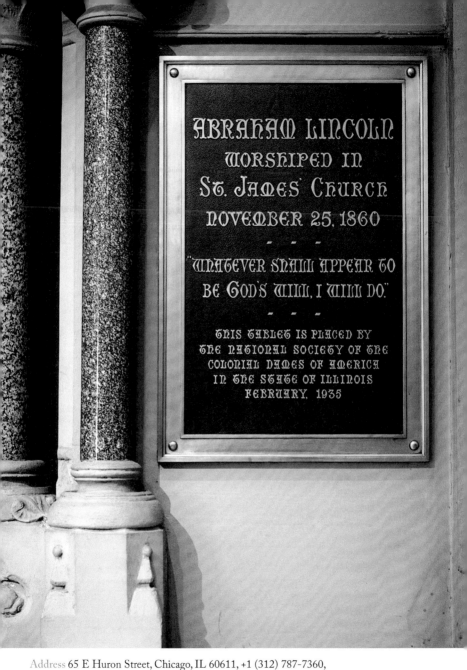

ABRAHAM LINCOLN
WORSHIPED IN
St. James' Church
NOVEMBER 25, 1860

- - -

"WHATEVER SHALL APPEAR TO
BE GOD'S WILL, I WILL DO."

- - -

THIS TABLET IS PLACED BY
THE NATIONAL SOCIETY OF THE
COLONIAL DAMES OF AMERICA
IN THE STATE OF ILLINOIS
FEBRUARY, 1935

Address 65 E Huron Street, Chicago, IL 60611, +1 (312) 787-7360, www.saintjamescathedral.org | Getting there Train to Chicago (Red Line) | Hours See website for services and events schedule | Tip Take a moment to find inner peace by walking the cathedral's hidden outdoor labyrinth, located in the oasis-like plaza adjacent to St. James, at the corner of Huron and Rush Streets.

25 Coiled Serpent Mound
Echoes of the ancients

Built by Native Americans over thousands of years, the historic mounds scattered across the Midwest serve as silent witnesses to the sophisticated societies that once thrived here. From the towering Cahokia Mounds of the Mississippian cultures in Illinois, to the intricate effigy mounds in Wisconsin dating to 650–1200 CE, these earthworks were used for various purposes, including ceremonial, burial, and residential functions. Each mound reveals a deep connection to the land and a remarkable engineering prowess.

There were Indigenous mounds in the Chicago area, but they've all been destroyed over time. A late 19th-century Chicago map marks the spot on Oakdale Avenue and Wellington Street where a lizard-shaped mound, built between 800 and 1,000 CE, once stood before it was destroyed during the construction of the elevated Brown Line.

The coiled Serpent Mound in Horner Park aims to honor and revive the mound-building tradition. This impressive earthwork installation, located along the western banks of the Chicago River, is an homage to the ancestral practice of building mounds and is designed to educate the public about the rich cultural history of placemaking. The mound is a collaborative effort by Native American artist Santiago X, landscape architect Nilay Mistry, and the Chicago Public Art Group. It is part of a larger initiative to create a conceptual museum along a nine-mile trail called the 4000N. This trail includes another earthwork, Pokto Cinto (Serpent Twin), located on the banks of the Des Plaines River in Schiller Woods West.

"Mounds haven't been built in North America since the founding of the United States," said Santiago X. "Taking us out of the past tense and this archaeological speak was a motivation behind this project – to really empower contemporary indigeneity throughout the landscape, and really give us a tangible place."

Address 2741 W Montrose Avenue, Chicago, IL 60618, +1 (773) 478-3499, www.chicagopublicartgroup.org/project/serpent-mound | **Getting there** CTA bus 49 to Western/Montrose. The Coiled Serpent Mount is located just beyond the banks of the Chicago River and is immersed in Native prairie and woods. Climb to the top for a beautiful vista of the Chicago River | **Hours** Daily dawn–dusk | **Tip** Horner Park also offers free or low-fee classes for children and adults, including 3D printing, archery, ceramics, American Sign Language, and more, as well as classes for people with disabilities (www.chicagoparkdistrict.com/parks-facilities/horner-henry-park#Programs).

26_ Colleen Moore Fairy Castle

All that glitters is gold and miniature

Colleen Moore envisioned the ultimate enchanted fairy castle, filled with sumptuous, antique furnishings, dripping with diamond accents, alight with golden chandeliers, and resplendent in royal regalia. In its kitchen, the copper stove that once threatened to burn Hansel and Gretel alive now bakes a four-and-twenty-blackbird pie. King Arthur's round table, set with solid gold plates and cutlery, awaits its brave guests at the center of the tapestry-lined dining hall. Sleeping Beauty once slept in the master bedroom, her bedspread made of golden spiderwebs. In the library over 80 books, including the world's tiniest bible, wait patiently to be read. At the entrance, a magical coach waits to take a princess to a ball. It cost a staggering $500,000 to build this dreamy castle, the equivalent of $7 million in today's money. But don't plan on moving in just yet: this magnificent castle measures just nine square feet.

Colleen Moore was an early Hollywood silent-film star with a passion for miniatures. In 1928, she hired famed Hollywood architect and set designer Horace Jackson to create the floor plan and layout for her dream dollhouse, and hired art director and designer Harold Grieve, who had revamped Colleen Moore's personal, Bel Air mansion, to create elaborate interiors. Moore, not only an actress but also a savvy businesswoman, organized a national tour for the dollhouse to raise money for children's charities. The delightful dollhouse made its way across the US in toy departments of stores in major cities.

In 1949, the Fairy Castle made its final stop at the Museum of Science and Industry, where it now rests in a lower-level corner. See if you can spot the tiny cradle that sits on the rocking tree in the Magic Garden. Made with jewelry from her grandmother, this cradle was Colleen Moore's most cherished miniature *objet d'art*.

Address Museum of Science and Industry, Lower Level, 5700 S Lake Shore Drive, Chicago, IL 60637, +1 (773) 684-1414, www.msichicago.org | Getting there Train to 55th-56th-57th Street (Metra Electric and South Shore Line) | Hours Daily 9:30am–4pm; check website for extended hours and exceptions | Tip If Tom Thumb were to plan a Chicago move, he could take his pick between Colleen Moore's luxe Fairy Castle and the 68 Thorne Miniature Rooms at the Art Institute of Chicago. Conceived by Mrs. James Ward Thorne of Chicago and built between 1932 and 1940, these tiny rooms, constructed on a scale of one inch to one foot, showcase rich interiors ranging from the late 13th century to the 1930s (111 S Michigan Avenue).

27 Confederate Mound
Mass grave of Civil War prisoners

The largest mass grave in the western hemisphere, containing the remains of thousands of Confederate prisoners of war killed at Camp Douglas, is hidden in a quiet corner of the Great Grand Crossing neighborhood. The Confederate Mound Memorial, located in the southwest section of Oak Woods Cemetery, is the only recognition of the service, suffering, and death of the approximately 6,000 men who are buried beneath the 30-foot granite column.

From January 1863 until the end of the war in May 1865, Camp Douglas, which stood at the edge of the prairie on Chicago's South Side, served as a Union Army organizational and training camp for volunteer regiments and ultimately a detention camp for paroled Confederate prisoners pending their formal exchange for Union prisoners. With a death rate averaging 20 percent, it is estimated that more than 6,000 Confederate prisoners died in detention here from disease, starvation, and the bitter cold winters from 1862 through 1865. The bodies of the dead were originally buried at the City Cemetery near Lake Michigan in Lincoln Park, which was then abandoned. From 1865 to 1867, they were exhumed and re-interred in this mass grave, known as Confederate Mound.

Confederate Mound is an oval-shaped plot, located between Divisions 1 and 2 of Section K in the park-like cemetery. Capping the column is a bronze statue of a Confederate soldier, based on the painting Appomattox by John A. Elder. The bas-relief images at the base include A Soldier's Death Dream, which depicts a fallen soldier and his horse on the battlefield. The monument was designed by General John C. Underwood and dedicated on May 30, 1895 by President Grover Cleveland before an estimated 100,000 onlookers. Four cannons surround the monument, with 12 marble headstones placed between it and the northern cannon, to mark the graves of unknown Camp Douglas Union guards.

Address 1035 E 67th Street, Chicago, IL 60637, +1 (773) 288-3800 | Getting there Train to Stoney Island (Metra Electric Line) | Hours Daily dawn–dusk | Tip While you're at Oak Woods Cemetery, pay your respects to other notable residents, including Chicago Mayor Harold Washington, crime boss Giacomo "Big Jim" Colosimo, Olympian Jesse Owens, civil rights activist Ida B. Wells, and physicist Enrico Fermi.

28 Couch Mausoleum

A stately reminder of a graveyard past

Strolling through lovely Lincoln Park with its flowers, verdant fields, ponds, and pathways, it is hard to believe that there are thousands of people buried beneath your feet.

Yet the southern edge of this lakefront park did indeed serve as the city cemetery. During the 19th century, Chicago buried its dead at the many religious graveyards and family-owned gravesites here, while the Potter's Field, located where the park's baseball diamond is today, welcomed indigent souls. It wasn't until 1864, after a doctor declared that it was unsafe to bury the dead so close to the lake, where bodily fluids and bacteria could so easily ooze out from the graves below to the water table, that city officials decided to relocate the bodies and turn this tranquil tract of land into a park. Workers transferred many of the deceased to other city cemeteries, but it was far too costly and difficult to remove the Couch Mausoleum, with its heavy stones fastened tightly together with copper rivets.

Ira Couch arrived in Chicago from New York in 1836. A tailor by trade, wise land and real estate acquisitions made him an early Chicago millionaire. He died in 1857, while wintering in Cuba, and his body was shipped back to Chicago, where he was entombed in this iron-fenced mausoleum, only his last name carved in stone over the vault's entrance. Other family members were likely later interred in this the family tomb, but no one knows exactly who rests eternally beside Ira.

In 1998, workers digging the site for the adjacent Chicago History Museum's parking garage in Lincoln Park (1731 N Clark Street) discovered the remains of more than 80 people, including one perfectly preserved in a sealed, 19th-century iron coffin. Ira Couch may or may not rest alone in his iron-gated tomb, but certainly many of his unmoved contemporaries still lie buried near him in the surrounding park.

Address Southwest corner of Lincoln Park, near N Clark Street and W LaSalle Drive, Chicago, IL | Getting there Train to Sedgwick (Brown and Purple Line) | Hours Unrestricted | Tip A boulder of Wisconsin granite marks the grave of David Kennison, the only other visible clue to Lincoln Park's graveyard past, near N Clark Street and Wisconsin Street. Though many doubt Kennison's outrageous claims, he declared himself the last survivor of the Boston Tea Party, a scout for George Washington, a survivor of both the Battle of Bunker Hill and the massacre at Fort Dearborn – and the Daughters of the American Revolution stand by him. A plaque on the boulder states that he died at the whopping age of 115 years, 3 months and 17 days.

29 __ Couch Place
Death alley

Couch Place, an unassuming alley nestled in the heart of Chicago's bustling Theater District, holds a dark and tragic secret. On December 30, 1903, a stage light in the adjacent Iroquois Theatre sparked and ignited a muslin curtain during a matinee performance of the musical *Mr. Blue Beard.* The flames quickly spread to the scenery and sets. When a backdraft launched a fireball through the theater packed with 1,700 patrons, the scene turned to utter mayhem. Nellie Reed, an aerialist performing in the musical, perished while suspended in her harness above the smoke-obscured stage below.

As the flames consumed the theater, desperate attempts to escape led many to Couch Place. The fire escapes were frozen and unusable, forcing people to jump from the upper floors into the alley below. Bodies piled up as those who leaped were cushioned by the fallen before them. The alley became a makeshift morgue, with over 600 people, dead and dying, strewn across the cobblestones. Most of the dead were women and children, who did not expect to meet their end while attending a musical about a legendary pirate known for his blue-hued beard.

Today, Couch Place stands as a somber reminder of that fateful day. Visitors to the alley often report eerie sensations, from faint cries and whispers to the feeling of being touched or pushed by unseen forces. The ghostly presence of those who perished in the fire lingers, adding an unsettling atmosphere to this otherwise ordinary alley.

The Iroquois Theatre fire led to significant changes in fire safety regulations and building codes. The next time you step inside a theater, note the doors that open outward to facilitate easier evacuation and the clearly illuminated exit signs. And remember the victims of the Iroquois Theatre fire, who lost the battle with the deadly fire but ultimately made theaters safer for all of us today.

Address 24 W Randolph Street, Chicago, IL 60601 | Getting there Train to Lake Street (Red Line) | Hours Unrestricted | Tip Five years after the fire, the Iroquois Theater Memorial Association dedicated a solemn granite monument at Montrose Cemetery (5400 N Pulaski Road, www.montrosecemetery.com/about/about). The stone marks the final resting place of the last unidentified victim of the fire, a woman in her fifties. The inscription reads, "Sacred to the memory of 600 people who perished in the Iroquois Theater Fire Dec. 30, 1903."

30 Coyote Building Rooftop
Romantic nook with glorious views

Near the Damen stop on the Chicago "L." at the intersection of Damen, North, and Milwaukee Avenues, the 12-story "flatiron," or wedge-shaped Northwest Tower, rose in 1929, attracting attorneys, doctors, and other professional offices mere months before the stock market crash brought the economy to a screeching halt. It wasn't until the 1980s that the building buzzed with activity once again. It became home to the Tower Coyote Gallery, reportedly named because artists thought the building resembled a howling coyote. In 2017, the building was restored back to its Art Deco glory when it reopened as the Robey Hotel.

For one of the most unique perspectives of the city, take an elevator up 203 feet to the 13th floor of the Coyote Building, the tallest building in the surrounding Wicker Park neighborhood, to the Up Room. Stretch out across low sofas next to the bar, or venture outside to the terrace where you'll see sweeping, windswept, 180-degree views of the neighborhood's tree-lined streets, the L train zipping along its steel tracks from the Damen Avenue station below, and a unique, eastward view of the city skyline in the near distance. You can even venture inside the cozy nook concealed in the Robey's spire, perhaps the perfect spot for a romantic nightcap in the city. Your rendezvous spot is even guarded by Art Deco knights with epic sword motifs carved into the concrete.

In the late 20th century, Chicago's burgeoning grunge culture took root here in Wicker Park. Music venues, such as Subterranean, redefined the city's music scene, attracting some of the world's most well-known bands, including the Rolling Stones, who played an epic $7 per ticket surprise concert at the Double Door in September 1997. On the Robey Hotel's second floor, Clever Coyote transports guests back to the grunge era, with its alt-rock soundtrack and vintage video games.

Address 1600 N Milwaukee Avenue, Chicago, IL 60647, +1 (872) 315-3084, www.therobey.com | Getting there Train to Damen (Blue Line) | Hours Up Room: Sun–Thu 5pm–midnight, Fri & Sat 5pm–1am | Tip The Robey Hotel took over the adjacent historic Hollander Storage Building and constructed the Cabana Club (1616 N Milwaukee Avenue, www.therobey.com), a rooftop hangout centered by a triangular pool where frozen cocktails flow.

31 Doane Observatory

Spy on galaxies far, far away

If you've ever dreamed of spying on the farthest galaxies in the universe – even trillions of miles away – the Doane Observatory, almost hidden on the shores of Lake Michigan just east of the Adler Planetarium's main building, promises to show you distant, celestial objects. Built in 1977, the observatory houses one of the nation's few astronomical telescopes located in a major city. The Doane's classical, 500-plus-pound Cassegrain reflector, together with its 20-inch-diameter mirror, gather over 5,000 times more light than an unaided human eye, allowing for long focal lengths and potentially high magnifications despite its relatively short telescope tube.

The Doane is constantly in motion – at the same rate as the earth rotates – from atop its banana-yellow, fork-style equatorial mounting. This movement keeps celestial objects centered in the field of view at all times so they can be watched for extended periods of time, although special limit switches prevent it from rotating in a full circle. If you've ever wanted to spot sunspots, the Doane also houses a Coronado SolarMax 90 hydrogen-alpha telescope and a dense filter for the "white-light" telescope, so you can stare directly into the sun.

Climb the small spiral staircase into the dome that houses the telescope, then climb another metal staircase, peer into the aperture and prepare to be amazed. Despite the bright city lights, the views to the east over Lake Michigan are strikingly clear.

The Doane Observatory is open for daytime telescope views of the sun from 10am to 1pm every day, weather permitting. Inquire at the box office when you arrive at the Adler Planetarium or call ahead to see if it will be open the day of your planned visit. Note that since use of the observatory is highly dependent on weather conditions and volunteer schedules, the daily schedule may change at a moment's notice.

Address 1300 S Lake Shore Drive, Chicago, IL 60605, +1 (312) 922-7827, www.adlerplanetarium.org | **Getting there** Train to Roosevelt (Red, Orange, and Green Line), then CTA bus 146 at State & Roosevelt Road | **Hours** Mon, Tue, Thu–Sun 9am–4pm, Wed 4–10pm | **Tip** Don't miss the opportunity to step into Adler Planetarium's historic Atwood Sphere, Chicago's oldest large-scale mechanical planetarium, constructed in 1913. Step into the slowly rotating, 17-feet-diameter sphere and watch as the brightest stars of the night sky appear via the 692 holes in its metal surface. Pilots once learned to navigate the nighttime sky from the comfort of this sphere.

32 Dovetail Brewery
The magic behind the beer

Hidden on a corner of Belle Plaine Avenue, wild Chicago-born yeast blows in through the third-floor window of the Dovetail Brewery, magically turning water into some of the best Lambic-style beers in Chicago. This microbrewery's sublime German-style Lager, Bavarian-style Hefeweizen, Franconian-style Rauchbier, and Vienna-style Lager are brewed with the same traditional methods that produce the kind of beers found in small, family-run breweries in Europe. The water is filtered and formulated for each beer; the malt sourced from specialty maltsters in Franconia; and the raw wheat drawn directly from farmers within 150 miles of Chicago.

Co-founders Hagen Dost and Bill Wesselink, both from Chicago, met at beer school in Munich. They returned to Chicago with a plan: to produce beer of the highest quality, similar to the level of craftsmanship found in fine, old-school woodworking. They named their beloved brewery Dovetail, after the dovetail joint, a classic symbol of quality and craftsmanship.

See how beer bubbles to life with a brewery tour, held every Saturday beginning at 11am. You'll taste the malt, feel the hops run through your fingers, see everything from a 120-plus-year-old copper mash from the 1000-year-old Weihenstephan pilot brewery in Germany, to a magnificent, custom-built koelschip, and sample three beers as you wander through the 22,000-square-foot facility. If you're lucky, a proud Dost will be your guide.

Outside of the brewery, you'll be hard-pressed to find the highly sought-after small batch brews. Dovetail self-distributes its beer in kegs, focusing on major beer venues in Chicago and other locations in the immediate vicinity within two miles of the brewery. The in-brewery Tap Room is family- and dog-friendly and guests are welcome to bring their own food (BYOF), making it the perfect spot to sip a flight of Dovetail's flagship brews.

Address 1900 W Belle Plaine Avenue, Chicago, IL 60613, +1 (773) 683-1414, www.dovetailbrewery.com | Getting there Train to Irving Park (Brown Line) | Hours Mon–Thu noon–10pm, Fri & Sat noon–11pm, Sun noon–8pm; see website for tour schedule | Tip Food trucks roll up curbside to Dovetail Brewery on a weekly basis, making it easier than ever to pair beer with your fave food truck delights. Check the event page at www.dovetailbrewery.com/events for upcoming food truck visits and more.

33 — Estereo's Mirror Bathroom
Disco in the loo

Once upon a time, Chicago's Milwaukee Avenue served as a vital trade route for Native American tribes, including the Ottawa, Chippewa, and Potawatomi. This centuries-old path was used for travel and trade, connecting different tribal regions and facilitating the exchange of goods and culture. By the 1830s, it had evolved into the Northwestern Plank Road and continued to facilitate trade and travel between Chicago and the northwest townships. Today, Milwaukee Avenue remains a vital artery of Chicago, reflecting its rich history and continuous evolution.

As automobiles became more popular, car dealerships and auto-related businesses popped up along this particular stretch of Milwaukee Avenue. By the 1920s, the street was lined with showrooms and service stations, catering to the growing demand for cars, a trend that continued through the mid-20th century. Milwaukee Avenue became known as "Automobile Row." Logan Square Auto Company opened here in the early 1920s and showcased some of the earliest car models from Ford and Chevrolet, while Milwaukee Avenue Motors, established in the late 1920s, specialized in luxury cars, including brands like Cadillac and Lincoln.

Estereo, located in Logan Square, is an all-day bar known for its agave-forward cocktails and lively Latin American vibe. Roll-up garage doors create a bright, airy space, while locals line up at the bar's triangle-shaped counter to sip expertly crafted cocktails made with spirits like pisco, cachaça, rum, tequila, and mezcal.

Estereo also houses the coolest bathroom in Chicago. Covered in mirrored disco ball tiles creating a dazzling, reflective space, this bathroom will transport you back to the 1970s, a quirky feature that perfectly complements the bar's lively atmosphere inspired by Latin America. Be sure to take a quick trip to the loo and enjoy a solo disco party.

Address 2450 N Milwaukee Avenue, Chicago, IL 60647, +1 (773) 360-8363, www.estereochicago.com | Getting there Train to Logan Square (Blue Line) | Hours Mon 5pm–2am, Tue–Fri & Sun noon–2am, Sat noon–3am | Tip The Comfort Station is a cozy cottage built in the early 1900s on Logan Square as a place for trolley riders to rest during their journey. Today, it functions as a community art space, hosting various events and exhibitions (2579 N Milwaukee Avenue, www.comfortstationlogansquare.org).

34 Fantasy Costumes

Reveal your true identity

Are you in urgent need of a gorilla suit? A latex mask of (jailed) former governor Rod Blagojevich? A Cheshire cat headpiece? An adhesive handlebar mustache? A George Washington-style colonial era wig? Fishnet stockings that fit a 350-pound person? Fantasy Costumes has you covered. This amazing, oversized shop, located in the historic Six Corners shopping district, offers an entire city block packed with over one million fanciful outfits as well as wigs, masks and makeup for every season and creative reason.

What started out as a small wigs-only store morphed into one of the biggest costume shops in the world as owner George Garcia gradually took over neighboring storefronts on this stretch of Milwaukee Avenue, and gathered an inventory that promises to costume customers from head to toe. More of a costume mall than a shop, Fantasy Costume's 18,000 square feet of floor space guarantee you'll find everything you need to become any character or beast.

With thousands of new items added each year, it's easy to get lost among the merchandise, which fills every corner, nook, cranny, and crevice from floor to ceiling. October during Halloween season, which accounts for about 40 percent of annual sales, it can be especially difficult to make your way around the many crowded rooms, each dedicated to a costume element. But the creative team members here, who are also known to hide behind boxes and pop out to scare customers, will point you in the right direction. In the two weeks leading up to the scariest day of the year, Fantasy Costumes is conveniently open 24 hours a day.

This is a place where anyone can find the tools and tricks they need to embrace even their most outlandish fantasies. Fantasy Costumes' mission hasn't changed over the last five decades: "We strive to help customers look great while having fun. And it's OK to get a little crazy."

Address 4065 N Milwaukee Avenue, Chicago, IL 60641, +1 (773) 777-0222, www.fantasycostumes.com | Getting there Train to Montrose (Blue Line) | Hours Mon–Fri 8:30am–7pm, Sat 9:30am–6pm, Sun 11am–5pm | Tip Also located at Six Corners, the 1,938-seat Portage Theater stands as one of the oldest movie houses in Chicago. Its annual organist-accompanied Silent Film Festival, hosted every August, is not to be missed (4050 N Milwaukee Avenue, www.theportagetheater.com).

35 Fern House

The Midwest as it was 300 million years ago

If you're looking to escape the brutal Chicago winter, fly away to the Garfield Park Conservatory, the perfect tropical vacation spot within the city during the winter months. At 4.5 acres, this botanical treasure is one of the largest greenhouse conservatories in the United States. Its lush, verdant Fern House offers not only a warm, welcome respite from the polar vortex, but also a glimpse of what the Midwest might have looked like millions of years ago.

Located in the midst of historic Garfield Park on Chicago's West Side, the conservatory was designed by renowned Prairie-style landscape architect Jens Jensen, and opened to the public in 1907. Jensen's goal of recreating naturalistic landscapes under the glass top, a revolutionary idea at the time, is nowhere more evident than in the Fern House, where primitive plants – plants that grew during the age of the dinosaurs, about 300 million years ago – rest on rocky outcroppings and surround a koi-filled lagoon.

Wandering among the cycads, which are ancient cone-bearing plants, ferns, mosses and liverworts, one would expect an acrotholus to pop out at any minute. Cycads can live up to 500 years, and some of the ones in this room are estimated to be over 300 years old. There are few flowers in the Fern House, since ferns don't have seeds or flowers: gently lift the fern's fronds and look at their undersides to see if you can spot the spores, single cell organisms that grow on these undersides, forming a wide variety of intricate patterns. Dispersed by wind, when a spore lands in the right environment, a new fern is born.

The waterfall at the back of this room is a reminder of Jens Jensen's unique, perfectionist vision for this particular house of the conservatory: he forced his mason to build and rebuild the bubbling waterfall several times until the falling water trickled to the beat of Mendelssohn's Spring Song.

Address Garfield Park Conservatory, 300 N Central Park Avenue, Chicago, IL 60624, +1 (312) 746-5100, www.garfieldconservatory.org | **Getting there** Train to Conservatory-Central Park Drive (Green Line) | **Hours** Wed 10am–8pm, Thu–Sun 10am–5pm | **Tip** The Elizabeth Morse Genius Children's Garden, located within the conservatory, features climbable leaves, a giant seed pod, a long, curvy slide and best of all, a chance to run around and breathe in oxygen–without a coat, hat, and gloves.

36 Fountain Girl
Water not whisky

Turn-of-the-century Chicago was a boozing and brawling city. A group of women, sick and tired of dealing with all the drinking, banded together to form the Woman's Christian Temperance Union (WCTU). They fought to provide groundbreaking social services to women who had to suffer from the fallout from chronic alcoholism. They established lodging houses, daycare centers for children of working women, a medical dispensary, kindergartens and Sunday schools – all groundbreaking public services at a time when heavy drinking was almost the norm among the working class. Though they were not strictly prohibitionist, the union did fight for social-reform agendas related to liquor. In a quiet corner of Lincoln Park, a bronze statue of a little girl offering water is a reminder of the struggle these women endured in the face of rampant alcohol abuse. The women's very own children saved up their pennies and nickels to pay for the Fountain Girl.

Water trickles down from the Fountain Girl's bronze cup, which resembles the badge of the Temperance Union, into a stone basin below. Horses once lapped up the water from the basin; today it is a popular spot for thirsty dogs.

The Fountain Girl's innocence, portrayed in her simple dress and bare feet, betray her true age and background. The 4.5-foot-tall little girl has moved around the city several times and even went missing for a spell that lasted 60 years. Her first job was to provide a healthy alternative to liquor – fresh water – to visitors at the World's Columbian Exposition in 1893. She lived in Jackson Park, the Loop, and then Lincoln Park, until she was stolen in 1958. The Chicago Park District tracked down a copy of the statue in Portland, Maine and molded her back into life once again in 2012. She is named in memory of suffragist and noted feminist Frances Willard, who served as the second president of the WCTU.

Address South of W LaSalle Drive and east of Chicago History Museum | Getting there Train to Sedgwick (Brown and Purple Line) | Hours Wed 10am–8pm, Thu–Sun 10am–5pm | Tip The Frances Willard House, once the home of Frances Willard and her family as well as the longtime headquarters of the Woman's Christian Temperance Union, is now a museum dedicated to Willard, one of history's most forward-thinking women (1730 Chicago Avenue, Evanston, www.franceswillardhouse.org).

37 __ Fountain of Youth

Pump your way to vitality

People have been searching the world forever for the magical fountain of youth, the elusive spring that promises to preserve the vigor and vitality of anyone who drinks or bathes in its waters. Conquistador Juan Ponce de León may have searched high and low throughout the New World for the legendary fountain, but he never thought to look in Chicago's Schiller Woods Forest Preserve, located just off Irving Park Road.

On any given day, you will find people lugging their multiple jugs to the creaky, metal, hand-operated pump that allegedly flows with the hallowed waters of well-being and longevity. The mysterious fount, which was first installed in 1945, could use a little rejuvenation itself, as it takes much muscle and a whole lot of squeaking to pull the water up from the extraordinary aquifer located 80-plus feet below the ground.

Though chemical analysis insists this is your typical water from a deep well, ask any bottle-bearing believer here and they'll tell you: this water not only tastes better, but it will make you feel better too. The mineral count is indeed higher than your standard tap water, with markedly low levels of iron and no added fluoride or chlorine. But despite the claims of the pump's faithful followers, no one has been able to determine if the water will keep you alive and kicking forever. It is indeed safe, as it is tested by the Illinois Department of Public Health for potentially harmful bacteria and other contaminants. It also tastes outstanding, with no metallic aftertaste whatsoever, but for a slight, smooth sulfur finish to remind you of its powers.

No matter the season, the weather, or the time of day, the Schiller Woods fountain's faithful are willing to stand in the lengthy line to get their fill of the mysterious waters. Bring a jug or two and get ready to pump your way towards eternal youth.

Address N Cumberland Avenue and W Irving Park Road, www.fpdcc.com/schiller-woods |
Getting there Train to Irving Park (Blue Line), then CTA bus 80 to Cumberland & Irving
Park | Hours Unrestricted | Tip The Fountain of Youth is located on the south side of Irving
Park Road, just west of Cumberland Avenue. After you've loaded up on longevity, head over
to the model airplane flying field, just east of the fountain, where enthusiasts wield not just
small-scale planes but also UFO-like drones and helicopters.

38 Full Moon Fire Jam

Dancing by the light of the moon

When the full moon appears and looms over Lake Michigan, a fire ignites within the hearts of the creative people who gather on the sandy beach just south of Foster Avenue. Post-sunset, fire dancers light up the beach to the beat of the gathered percussionists; blazing poi, staffs, and hula hoops mesmerize the fans of the bewitching Full Moon Fire Jam, a magical, moonlit reverie. If you can't make it out to Black Rock City, the Full Moon Fire Jam that unfolds along the sandy beach is as close as you'll get to the Burning Man in Chicago.

What started in 2004 with a group of friends coming together to celebrate a birthday has grown into a free monthly celebration that draws one of the most diverse crowds in the city. The mission sounds lofty – "to unite performing artists and spectators through a love and appreciation of fire art" – but the end product is a friendly jam that goes beyond its main objective by uniting people of all ages, backgrounds and interests, from local Burners to casual passersby who find themselves mesmerized by the melding of artistry and athleticism that is performance fire art.

Full Moon Fire Jams take place on the night of each full moon falling between Sundays and Thursdays, from late spring to late fall. Performances take place south of the Foster Avenue Turf Fields, on the lakefront near the 5100 block of N Lake Shore Drive. They begin at sundown and end at 10pm. The jams are volunteer-run, not-for-profit, free to attend, family- and pet-friendly gatherings that follow the "Ten Principles of Burning Man": radical inclusion, gifting, decommodification, radical self-reliance, radical self-expression, communal effort, civic responsibility, "leave no trace," participation, and immediacy. Be sure to arrive early to secure a space. And bring water, blankets, your positive energy and a djembe if you want to join the jam session.

Address Lakefront, near 5100 Block of N Lakeshore Drive, www.fullmoonjam.org | Getting there Train to Argyle (Red Line) | Hours Late spring–late fall; on full moon nights falling Sun–Thu, sunset–10pm | Tip If you want to learn how to dance with fire, literally, Pyrotechniq Chicago offers both small and large group workshops as well as private lessons in the fine art of fire spinning in their flow dojos across the city (www.pyrotechniq.org/fire-dancing-lessons).

39 Ghost Church Façade
Halfway home for lost souls

At the corner of 19th and Peoria in Pilsen, an eerie, Old Chicago church beckons any lost souls to enter through its heavy wooden doors for a moment of respite and prayer. If you hear the bell in the 90-foot-tall tower toll, you'll know you've made your way into an altogether more spiritual dimension. Step inside the Ghost Church and you'll discover that there is no actual church behind the façade, rather just a small patch of grass and a few remaining stones from the foundation level that once supported a vibrant church.

The German Gothic script above the entrance lets you know that this was once the Zion Evangelical Lutheran Church. The congregation that built it was founded in Pilsen East in 1850, and then the church itself was built in the 1880s. When the last of the German-American congregants moved out of their East Pilsen neighborhood in 1956, they sold their church. It remained shuttered from the community until a fire in 1979 gutted the interior, and then the walls were knocked down to the ground by a severe wind storm in 1998, leaving little else besides the front façade and the bell tower.

Developer John Podmajersky Jr. purchased the property prior to the windstorm. When a group of descendants of the original congregants visited him, they brought with them an old book written in German that contained the church's early history, and his heartstrings were officially tugged. Podmajersky proceeded to restore the building's original façade and bell tower, and he has maintained the ghostly church ever since. He has plans to turn the bell tower into 10 small studio spaces.

Though the sanctuary itself is gone, it is still possible to sit upon the foundation stones to contemplate life prayerfully, in front of the still charred statue of Christ that remains high on the back of the bare brick, steel-truss supported entrance wall.

Address 19th Street and S Peoria Street, Chicago, IL 60608 | **Getting there** Train to 18th (Pink Line) or CTA bus 62 to Halsted & 18th Street | **Hours** Unrestricted | **Tip** Kitty-corner from the Ghost Church you'll find Open Books, a browse worthy, nonprofit secondhand bookstore for kids and adults, with all proceeds dedicated to supporting community literacy programs (905 W 19th Street, www.open-books.org).

40　Graveface Records

Music meets the macabre

Ryan Graveface is the founder of Graveface Records, an independent record label best known for its eclectic and experimental catalog, and a musician in bands such as Black Moth Super Rainbow, Dreamend, The Marshmallow Ghosts, and The Casket Girls. He moved into a little coach house in the Norwood Park neighborhood, near serial killer John Wayne Gacy's former abode, in 2007. "I started to have all these daily interactions with people who knew him in some capacity or claimed they knew him in some capacity," said Graveface in a 2023 interview with WUSC 90.5FM. Graveface acquired a painting the serial killer made in jail, as well as detailed notebooks.

Chicago, with its fiery music scene and supportive community, provided an ideal environment for Graveface to explore his passion for music and oddities. He opened Graveface Records in 2022. Stacks of new and used records encompass genres like shoegaze, dream pop, psych, experimental, and garage rock, as well as exclusive releases from their in-house labels Terror Vision and Never Not Goth.

The in-store Graveface Museum features a collection of true crime artifacts, sideshow memorabilia, and other curiosities. Enter through a banner depicting the Devil's mouth. Of particular note are the many John Wayne Gacy items, including paintings like his unsettling *Seven Dwarves* series, and documents that shed light on the infamous serial killer, including an early, handwritten interrogation of a boy who got away from his clasp. The mini-museum showcases a one-of-a-kind collection of sideshow memorabilia related to the unusual acts that captivated crowds at the 1933 Chicago World's Fair, including The Alligator Boy and Madame Zola, the Bearded Lady, and the office effects of Anton LaVey, founder of the Church of Satan. Descend into the depths of the basement to try your luck on the spookiest arcade games in the city.

Address 1829 N Milwaukee Avenue, Chicago, IL 60647, +1(912) 335-8018, www.graveface.com, mail@graveface.com | Getting there Train to Western Avenue (Blue Line) | Hours Wed–Sat noon–7pm, Sun 11am–7pm | Tip After exploring the museum, walk over to Irazu (1865 N Milwaukee Avenue, www.irazuchicago.com) for Costa Rican cuisine, including the best *patacones* (deep-fried plantains) and iced horchata coffee in the city.

41 Gwendolyn Brooks' Outdoor Office

The oracle of Bronzeville

In 1967, Richard Daley, then mayor of Chicago, asked Gwendolyn Brooks to write a poem to commemorate the dedication of the Chicago Picasso, the enormous, often misunderstood, pigeon like steel sculpture that still stands in Daley Plaza downtown. Her poem is perhaps best remembered for the line, "Art urges voyages – and it is easier to stay at home."

Gwendolyn Brooks chose the more difficult path – to create the art that urges voyages – as she captured the vitality of her beloved neighborhood, Bronzeville, the cultural hub of Black America, throughout her prolific writing career.

Born in Topeka, Kansas on June 7, 1917, Brooks was raised in Chicago and lived here until her death on December 3, 2000. A prolific writer, she was the author of more than twenty books of poetry, including Children Coming Home (The David Co., 1991); Annie Allen (Harper, 1949), for which she received the Pulitzer Prize; and A Street in Bronzeville (Harper & Brothers, 1945). She also wrote a novel, Maud Martha (Harper, 1953) and a memoir, Report from Part One: An Autobiography (Broadside Press, 1972). In 1968, she was named Poet Laureate for the State of Illinois, and in 1985, she was the first Black woman appointed as Consultant in Poetry to the Library of Congress, a post now known as United States Poet Laureate.

This new park, inaugurated in 2018 and located less than one mile from her childhood home at 4332 South Champlain, celebrates Brooks, "the oracle of Bronzeville," and includes a sculpted bust of Brooks, a stepping stone path etched with quotations from Annie Allen, and a stone circle. Step into her "outdoor office," and take a moment to sit on the porch modeled after the poet's childhood writing spot for a glimpse into Brooks' unique perspective on Bronzeville.

Address 4532 S Greenwood Avenue, Chicago, IL 60653, +1 (312) 747-7138, www.chicagoparkdistrict.com/parks-facilities/brooks-gwendolyn-park | Getting there Train to 47th St. (Metra Kenwood Line) | Hours Daily dawn–dusk | Tip While in Bronzeville, pay a visit to the Monument to the Great Northern Migration (345 E Eastgate Place). Sculptor Alison Saar created this bronze figure as a testament to the thousands of African Americans who migrated to Chicago in the early 20th century in search of freedom and opportunity.

42 The Highest Natural Point
Chicago from prairie to peak

Long ago, during the Wisconsin Glaciation, a colossal glacier swept across the land, carving out a grand basin that would one day become the sparkling Lake Michigan. As the glacier melted, its waters filled the basin, creating a shimmering lake that glistened under the sun. In this enchanted realm, the City of Chicago arose, perched upon the Chicago Plain, once the bed of the ancient Lake Chicago. The land was so flat and smooth that even the tiniest hills and ridges stood out like majestic peaks.

The highest natural point in Chicago, known as the morainal ridge of Blue Island, reaches an elevation of 672 feet above sea level and is located at the intersection of 91st Street and Western Avenue in the Dan Ryan Woods, an area historically known as Blue Island, named for its appearance as an island in a sea of prairie grass. The significance of this point lies not only in its elevation but also in its historical context: Blue Island served as a notable landmark for early settlers and traders navigating the vast, flat landscape of the region. Today, it remains a prominent feature in the Beverly neighborhood, offering a unique vantage point of the city skyline in the distance and a glimpse into the city's natural topography.

On snowy days, the hilltop that marks the highest natural point echoes laughter and excitement as people of all ages enjoy the crisp winter air and the thrill of speeding down the slope on a sled. At the bottom of the hill, a charming warming house centered by a roaring fire awaits.

It's easy to spot the highest peak in the preserve, and it's an easy walk to the hilltop from the Visitors Center parking lot. See if you can spot the large boulder, hidden in the woods to the side of the hilltop, which once marked the highest natural point in the city. It was later moved to make way for winter sports enthusiasts. Don't forget to bring a sled on snowy days!

Address 8700 S Western Avenue, Chicago, IL 60620, +1 (800) 870-3666, www.fpdcc.com/
places/locations/dan-ryan-woods | Getting there CTA bus 87 to 2600 W 87th Street |
Hours Daily dawn–dusk | Tip Robert Givins' Irish Castle (10244 S Longwood Drive,
www.chicagosonlycastle.org) is a three-story, 19th-century structure with crenelated towers
located in Chicago's Beverly neighborhood. Built between 1886 and 1887, it has served as a
private residence and a college. Today, it's a Unitarian church.

43 Insect Asylum
Make friends with bugs, butterflies, and beetles

Creepy crawlies aren't so creepy after all, once you learn the fascinating natural history behind their sometimes hair-raising appearance. Get up close and personal with moths, scorpions, birds, butterflies, beetles, praying mantises, and more at Insect Asylum, a mini-museum tucked along bustling Milwaukee Avenue.

Owner Nina Salem grew up in a quaint Massachusetts town and was long fascinated with collecting rocks, bones, and feathers. She also rescued animals and wildlife, eventually delving into taxidermy. She hid her passion for years, fearing being labeled as an "oddball." Today, she curates the collection of over 4,500 meticulously crafted taxidermy specimens and captivating live insect exhibits.

Unlike larger museums, this collection / community space is hands-on and touch-friendly for the most part. Feel free to touch items marked with a green dot. All the taxidermy specimens are ethically sourced, too, so you know the cicada, spider, or ladybug you're meeting died a natural death. Among the items displayed here are a mummified stingray, historically used to ward off demons and dragons, a taxidermy giraffe, and Hazel, a living opossum who resides at the museum full-time. When she's feeling up to it, the Asylum hosts special meet-and-greet sessions, where visitors can interact with her.

The Asylum also offers a wide range of interactive and educational experiences, including entomology pinning workshops, where you can learn how to pin and preserve butterflies and beetles; cat-themed acoustic jams; queer cicada yoga; and owl pellet dissection workshops, where you'll learn to craft jewelry or bookmarks with the tiny bones you dig out from owl regurgitation. The museum also hosts monthly, sensory-friendly workshops that combine fun and learning. The in-museum gift shop sells unique insect-themed art, home goods, and jewelry created by local artists.

Address 2870 N Milwaukee Avenue, Chicago, IL 60618, +1 (312) 961-7219, www.theinsectasylum.com, theinsectasylum@gmail.com | Getting there Train to Belmont (Blue Line) | Hours Thu–Sun 11am–8pm, Wed 3–8pm | Tip Chiya Chai (2770 N Milwaukee Avenue, www.chiyachai.com) serves 150+ possible combinations of freshly brewed chai tea, as well as Nepali and Indian-influenced food, including savory pies, steamed dumplings, and rich curries.

44 Institute for the Study of Ancient Cultures

Unleash your inner Indiana Jones

Where else can you pet a 40 ton human-headed winged bull, stare into the eyes of King Tutankhamen, or try your hand at interpreting the many spells contained in a papyrus segment from a Ptolemaic period *Book of the Dead.* The University of Chicago's Institute for Study of Ancient Cultures has been digging up treasures from faraway lands since 1919, amassing a collection that offers a unique glimpse into ancient civilizations lost to the sands of time.

Many point to Professor James Henry Breasted, founder of the Institute with funds donated by John D. Rockefeller, Jr., as the inspiration behind Indiana Jones. Though no reckless treasure hunter himself, Breasted was a committed field researcher with a knack for interpreting ancient writings, especially those from sources and structures that he feared may be lost forever. He even assisted Howard Carter in deciphering the seals from the Tomb of Tutankhamen.

Housed in an unusual Art Deco/Gothic building at the corner of 58th Street and University Avenue, the collection includes must-see oddities including an ear stella – a small tablet similar in size to an iPhone and believed to be a direct conduit to the Gods; a coffin containing a mummified lizard; and the mummy of forever-lovely Meresamun, a "Singer in the Interior of the Temple of Amun" at Karnak. The highlight of the collection is the enormous lamassu, a sculpture depicting a protective human-bull-bird spirit that once guarded the entrance to the throne room of King Sargon II. Viewed from the side, the creature appears to be walking; but when viewed from the front, it appears to be standing still.

Self-guided activities are available in both English and Spanish, including a popular treasure hunt. Don't forget to stop at the Suq, the charming in-museum gift shop.

Address The University of Chicago, 1155 E 58th Street, Chicago, IL 60637, +1 (773) 702-9520, www.oi.uchicago.edu | Getting there Train to 59th Street/University of Chicago (Metra Electric Line) | Hours Tue–Sun 10am–5pm (Wed until 8pm) | Tip Though now occupied by the Phi Gamma Delta frat, James Henry Breasted's Hyde Park home, designed to resemble the villa of Ariosto in Ferrara, Italy, features two ancient Egyptian-style serpents on either side of the front door (5615 S University Avenue).

45 Irish American Heritage Center

The heartbeat of Irish culture in Chicago

Irish immigration to Chicago began in the 1830s, with a significant influx during the Great Famine (1845–1849). By 1850, the Irish made up about one-fifth of Chicago's population, contributing to the city's growth through labor on canals and railroads, and in industries like meatpacking. They established strong communities and played influential roles in the city's Catholic Church and local politics. As Mary McAleese, former President of Ireland once said, "The immigrant's heart marches to the beat of two quite different drums, one from the old homeland and the other from the new. The immigrant has to bridge these two worlds, living comfortably in the new and bringing the best of his or her ancient identity and heritage to bear on life in an adopted homeland."

The Irish American Heritage Center is a cultural gathering space dedicated to preserving and promoting Irish heritage. Housed in the former Mayfair School building, the center features a theater, library, museum, art gallery, all adorned with stunning Celtic designs and murals. The center is a cornerstone for the local Irish community, hosting a variety of events, classes, and performances that celebrate Irish culture and traditions.

The library has an extensive collection of books, music, and the world's largest database of Irish newspapers, some dating back to 1738. A small museum boasts Belleek Parian China, a tapestry by Lily Yeats (sister of W. B. Yeats), a Victoria square piano, and a lovely collection of intricate Irish lace. But the gem of the center is its cozy Fifth Province Pub, designed with materials from the old school building, including a bar countertop made from chalkboards. When you gather around the pub's roaring fireplace for live music and a pint, you'll feel transported to Dublin.

Address 4626 N Knox Avenue, Chicago, IL 60630, +1(773) 282-7035, www.Irish-american.org | **Getting there** Train to Montrose (Blue Line) | **Hours** See website for events, programs, and library, gift shop, and pub hours | **Tip** The oldest Irish pub in Chicago is Shinnick's Pub (3758 S Union Avenue, www.shinnicks.com), which has been family-run since 1938. The beautiful, wooden back bar is believed to have been exhibited at the 1893 World's Fair.

46 Iwan Ries & Co.

Where King Tobacco still reigns

Chicago was once a smoking town, where most every man, rich or poor, cherished a long drag on a good cigar or pipe packed with fragrant tobacco. Today you would be hard pressed to find anyone smoking inside even the grittiest bar, thanks to the 2008 Smoke Free Illinois Act. But there is one secret Loop lounge where you can puff away to your heart's (dis)content on some of the finest tobacco blends in the world. At Iwan Ries' swanky lounge, cigars have staged their comeback, and pipe smoking is a practice that has never gone out of style.

Iwan Ries and Company has supplied smokers with tobacco, pipes, lighters, and many more accoutrements since 1857, making it the oldest family-owned tobacco shop in the country. Prepare to be enveloped in the heady smell of fine cigar and pipe tobacco as soon as the elevator opens to reveal this second-floor shop, located in the Adler and Sullivan designed Jewelers Building (1881). Rows upon rows of cigars line the glass cases, while over 15,000 pipes are displayed on the walls, include a noteworthy collection of antique pipes, snuff boxes, and lighters. Among the many different types of tobacco, the shop's signature blend – Three Star Blue – stands apart from all of the others.

Step into the private smoking lounge, sink into a leather chair, and take in both the fine tobacco and the fine views of bustling Wabash Avenue below, and the L as it snakes its way around the Loop before your eyes. The lounge managed to be grandfathered in when the city smoking ban went into effect, and hence stands as downtown Chicago's one and only smoking lounge. You can pay for a single entrance, or you can become a member for a marvelous set of benefits, including personal key-card access and invitations to private tastings and events. The lounge is BYOB, so bring a bottle of your favorite cognac or port; glassware is provided.

Address 19 S Wabash Avenue, Chicago, IL 60603, +1 (312) 372-1306, www.iwanries-hub.com | Getting there Train to Monroe (Red Line) or Randolph/Wabash (Brown, Green, Orange, Pink, and Purple Line) | Hours Mon–Fri 9am–5:30pm, Sat 9am–5pm | Tip Chicago's landmark Jewelers Row spans two blocks of Wabash Avenue, between E Washington Street and E Monroe Street, making it the most popular spot to choose a cherished engagement ring. At the Jewelers Center housed in the Mallers Building, a magnificent Art Deco structure built in 1912, you'll find over 180 independent jewelers under one roof (5 S Wabash Avenue, www.jewelerscenter.com).

47 — Johnny Weissmuller Pool
Tarzan's training grounds

The Medinah Athletic Club opened its doors in 1929 to much acclaim. Private and exclusive, this tony club was a posh playground for Chicago's rising rich and famous crowd. Over $5 million had been spent building the club's extravagant, Assyrian-inspired building, which stood at 42 stories and was capped with a Moorish-style golden dome, built to serve as a docking port for dirigibles. A miniature golf course, shooting range, billiard hall, running track, gymnasium, archery range, bowling alley, and a two-story boxing arena challenged the club's 3,000 members. On the 14th floor, the Johnny Weissmuller Pool shined, an Art Deco gem reminiscent of the Golden Age in Spain.

Best known for swinging into the role of Tarzan on the silver screen in the thirties and forties, Johnny Weissmuller was also a competitive swimmer with a number of records under his belt. When in Chicago, the Hollywood dreamboat dove into the exclusive swimming pool now named in his honor.

Ten feet at its deepest end, the pool's diving board is long gone, but you can still dive in after a busy day of shopping the Magnificent Mile with the purchase of a reasonably priced resort pass or as a hotel guest. Note the tin-glazed majolica tiles that line the blue-tiled pool's edge. The terracotta statue of Neptune on the eastern wall is surrounded by wide-mouthed fish fountains. When light shines through the windows, with their scale-shaped, aquamarine and sapphire stained glass, schools of fish are magically reflected onto the water. Swimming was once a popular spectator sport, so order a retro cocktail and lie back on one of the poolside wicker chaise lounges and imagine watching synchronized swimming icon Ester Williams gracefully diving in before your eyes, as she did in the 1940s, when the Johnny Weissmuller Pool was one of the most glamorous places to see and be seen in the city.

Address InterContinental Chicago, 505 N Michigan Avenue, Chicago, IL 60611, +1 (312) 944-4100, www.resortpass.com/hotels/intercontinental-chicago | Getting there Train to Grand (Red Line) | Hours See website for resort passes and guest events | Tip Head under N Michigan Avenue to the Billy Goat Tavern for post-swim beers and "Cheezborger, cheezborger, cheezborger, no fries, chips," a line immortalized by John Belushi in "Olympia Café," a hilarious *Saturday Night Live* sketch inspired by the tavern (430 N Michigan Avenue, lower level, www.billygoattavern.com).

48 Klairmont Kollections
Rolling works of art

Born in Chicago on December 17, 1926, Larry Klairmont's early life involved a string of odd jobs – Chinese food delivery, women's shoe sales – as he needed to help support his family. At just 16, he enlisted and served in World War II as a combat Marine in the brutal battles of Saipan and Iwo Jima. His valor earned him two Purple Hearts, two Silver Stars, and a Bronze Star. Post-war, Klairmont's determination led him to establish Imperial Cleaners, a 100-store dry cleaning chain that dominated Chicago until 1962. Then he found incredible success in real estate.

Klairmont always loved cars, and as soon as he had the means, he began collecting them. His love for cars transcended mere mechanics; it embraced the artistry, engineering marvels, and cultural impact of these rolling works of art. His car collection grew so big he decided to create a car museum of his very own. Today, his Klairmont Kollections Automotive Museum in Chicago houses over 300 historic vehicles. The rows upon rows of cars here seem to go on forever.

Step inside this 100,000-square-foot, gearhead wonderland adorned with vintage neon signs and eclectic collectibles, to admire classic roadsters, sleek sports cars, and some of the wackiest vehicles ever made, including a two-faced Ford, a car with two identical front ends welded back to back so its driver never needs to use reverse; a 1976 Cadillac Eldorado Convertible, a legendary concept car that averages a mere 10 miles per gallon; the 1954 Golden Sahara II; an ultra-elegant 1959 Cadillac Eldorado Biarritz Convertible; and a Pulse Litestar autocycle, an absurd vehicle with vestigial wings. This is also the only museum where you'll find a Nazi Bomber Plane that survived World War II, an early 20th century Chicago police lock-up van, a Batmobile, the Munsters Koach, and Shaggy's van from *Scooby Doo* all on display under the same roof.

Address 3117 N Knox Avenue, Chicago, IL 60641, +1 (773) 685-1904, www.klairmontkollections.com, info@klairmontkollections.com | Getting there Train to Clybourn (Red Line) | Hours Wed–Sun 10am–4pm | Tip The world's largest Radio Flyer wagon, constructed from a whopping six tons of steel, is on display outside Radio Flyer's 65,000-square-foot, LEED platinum-certified headquarters (6515 W Grand Avenue, www.radioflyer.com).

49 Leather Archives and Museum

Capturing a scintillating subculture

It holds one of the most interesting collections of artifacts in the city of Chicago, stands as the first and foremost museum of its kind, promises to provoke, challenge and engage – and yet few people even know that this fascinating museum exists. The Leather Archives and Museum delves deep into the fascinating BDSM culture and community. Its 10,000-square-foot building, located in Rogers Park, houses eight exhibitions, an extensive archival storage space, an auditorium, a library, and, of course, a veritable sex dungeon in its basement. The focus here is on bondage, discipline (or domination), sadism, and masochism (as a type of sexual practice), and on the leather subculture in all its glorious forms of expression. Many displayed treasures mark the subculture's journey out of the closet, from early beefcake mags to the flag carried by the Leather Contingent at the 25th anniversary of the Stonewall Riot in New York City. Leather culture sprouted up out of biker culture in the 1940s, when devotees dressed in leather garments – boots, chaps, harnesses, jackets – to separate themselves from the mainstream. The culture has found different expressions within the gay, lesbian, bisexual, and straight worlds, but it's most visible in gay communities. In addition to boasting the first leather museum of its kind in the world, Chicago plays host to the annual International Mr. Leather, the largest leather conference and contest in the world. The Windy City was also the home of the first gay leather bar, the Gold Coast, which opened its doors and many closed minds way back in 1958.

While many of the objects on display here lean towards the titillating – antique whips, chains, spanking machines, handcuffs, vintage leather fetish clothing – the stately museum is also home to extensive archives that document the history of this captivating counterculture.

Address 6418 N Greenview Avenue, Chicago, IL 60626, +1 (773) 761-9200, www.leatherarchives.org | Getting there Train to Loyola (Red Line) | Hours Thu & Fri 11am–7pm, Sat & Sun 11am–5pm | Tip Touché began welcoming leather lovers way back in 1977, and it remains one of the best leather fetish bars in the city (6412 N Clark Street, www.touchechicago.com).

50 Light Court at the Rookery

Illuminating from within

When it opened in 1885, the 11-story Rookery was seen as a soaring skyscraper, an engineering marvel. This once-tallest building in the city of Chicago cost a whopping $1.5 million and was considered the most elegant office building in the country. To this day, it remains a most sought-after address within the LaSalle Street financial corridor, and it stands as the oldest high-rise in the city. Step into the glorious, two-story light court with its glass ceiling, white-glazed brick walls, sublime light fixtures, and winding oriel staircase, and you'll see why it's considered one of architect Frank Lloyd Wright's grandest masterpieces. It was also his first major architectural job, and his only remaining work in downtown Chicago.

The Rookery's interior light court illuminates the building's square interior, designed by famed 19th-century Chicago architects John Wellborn Root and Daniel Burnham in 1888. Wright was hired in 1905 to remodel the steel-laden, glass-ceiling-topped lobby. He added all his meticulous, Prairie-style touches, including luxurious white marble with Persian-style ornamentation, intricate staircase railings, ornamented light fixtures, and the signature, decorative urns at the base of the staircase, creating a modernized design that maximized available light. Walk up the curving, heavily ornamented staircase which winds up from the 2nd floor, wrap-around balcony to the 12th floor, and you'll see why the light court at the Rookery was a place to see and be seen at the turn of the century.

The Rookery was named after the many pigeons and crows, a.k.a. rooks, that set up their nests on the building's exterior, and the shady politicians who worked in the post-fire City Hall that once stood on the site. See if you can spot the couple of rooks carved on the façade over the LaSalle Street entrance by architect John Root.

Address 209 S LaSalle Street, Chicago, IL 60604, +1 (312) 553-6100,
www.therookerybuilding.com | Getting there Train to Quincy/Wells (Brown, Orange,
Pink, and Purple Line) | Hours Light Court Lobby: Mon–Fri 7am–6pm, Sat 8am–2pm |
Tip You might recognize the Rookery from Home Alone 2: Lost in New York, in which the
exterior and one of the lower levels were modeled as the toy store, "Duncan's Toy Chest."
The building also starred in the 1987 film The Untouchables as the police headquarters
of Eliot Ness.

51 LondonHouse Cupola
Pop the question at the tiptop

If you are going to pop the question, do it here, 23 stories above street level in the open-air, cozy cupola of a landmark 1920s skyscraper. Majestic 360-degree views of the Chicago River and downtown will surround you as you toast to a new life together and sip champagne in the most exclusive private dining spot in the city.

Designed by Chicago architect Alfred S. Alschuler, the Beaux Arts London Guarantee & Accident Building stands at the south bank of the Chicago River, on the former site of Fort Dearborn. The fort itself was built in 1808 and played an important role in early Chicago history, as witness to a major battle in 1812. You will see a bronze relief depicting the famous fort above the building's main entrance on East Wacker Drive. Restored to its former glory and transformed into the LondonHouse Hotel in 2013, the property sold in 2016 for a cool $315 million, making it the highest per-room ever paid for a Chicago hotel, at $697,000 per room. The hotel's name is a tribute to the famous, eponymous first-floor nightclub that hosted some of the biggest names in jazz from the fifties through the early seventies.

The temple-like circular cupola, raised on an elaborate podium at the tippy top, is reminiscent of the glorious Choragic Monument of Lysicrates in Athens. Ringed with regal columns and capped with a cupola inscribed with an X and O pattern that is part of its original 1923 design, the intimate terrace seats only two. It seems to have been designed with romance in mind, making it Chicago's premier proposal site. The $1,000 price tag to rent this timeless perch includes everything you need to pop the question: a kneeler, a bottle of Dom Perignon, and a discount on a wedding, should you choose to celebrate your nuptials at the LondonHouse. A beaming "Yes!" is not guaranteed, but a starry night sky and glittering city lights are added bonuses.

Address 85 E Upper Wacker Drive, Chicago, IL 60601, +1 (312) 357-1200, www.londonhousechicago.com | Getting there Train to State / Lake (Brown, Green, Orange, Pink, and Purple Line) | Hours By reservation only | Tip The nearby Jewelers Building once featured car elevators that whisked jewelers concerned with their safety to private, secure parking garages on the lower 23 floors. During Prohibition, the building's magnificent dome held Al Capone's speakeasy, the Stratosphere Club. Check out the building's creepy corner clock, attached to the Wacker Drive façade, which features Father Time and his devilish scythe, outlined in blood red light bulbs (35 E Wacker Drive).

52 Maggie Daley Park Skating Ribbon

The cherry atop winter's cake

Gliding on the Maggie Daley Park Skating Ribbon is the cherry atop winter's cake. Merry skaters zoom along the quarter-mile-long, 20-foot-wide rink, while beginners hold tight to rails to make their skating experience a bit easier on the behind. This is the most beautiful spot in the city to skate your winter worries away and experience the joys of the season, especially in the evening, when the city's skyscrapers glow with holiday lights, the stars twinkle overhead, and the chill makes holding mittened hands with your loved ones not so much a necessity but a joy.

Located near the Lake Michigan shoreline in northeastern Grant Park, the 20-acre park, inaugurated in 2014, was named for Maggie Daley, the beloved former first lady of the city who died in 2011. The park features tennis courts, perhaps the most amazing playground in the city, picnic groves, and gorgeous gardens. In the summer, new and experienced climbers test their skills on the rock-climbing structures, which reach up to 40 feet. In the wintertime, the ribbon rink is abuzz with skaters. The many smiling kids that visit this city park are a happy reminder of Maggie Daley's love and hard work on behalf of Chicago's children.

Skate around the loop – twice the length of a lap around a traditional skating rink – then warm up with some hot cocoa in the adjacent warming house. The rink is closed for one-hour periods, during which the ice is resurfaced by a rambling Zamboni machine. Thankfully, this zesty Zamboni has a dedicated twitter account, @MDPZamboni, so you can make sure to arrive when the ice is at its smoothest.

When spring arrives and the ice melts away, the skating ribbon morphs into a paved, winding walking path where visitors are welcome to whiz around on roller skates.

Address 337 E Randolph Street, Chicago, IL 60601, +1 (312) 552-3000, www.chicagoparkdistrict.com/parks | **Getting there** Train to Millennium Station (Metra Electric and South Shore Line); train to Randolph/Wabash (Brown, Green, Orange, Pink, and Purple Line) | **Hours** See website for seasonal hours | **Tip** BomboBar is a walk-up window in the West Loop beloved for its delicious bomboloni (hole-less Italian doughnuts) and over-the-top hot chocolates. It's the perfect post-ice skating indulgence (832 West Randolph Street, www.bombobar.com).

53 The Magic Hedge
Ornithophiles' paradise

Blackburnian warblers and black-headed gulls. Snowy owls and saw-whets. Black-bellied plovers and semi-palmated sparrows. When these rare birds fly over Lake Michigan, they usually swoop down, stop, and stay for a while at a magical 15-acre lakeside sanctuary, where thick hedgerows, trees with hospitable branches, and dense thickets act as a five-star Chicago hotel for the birds.

Many birds love the Montrose Point Bird Sanctuary, also known as the Magic Hedge, a small tree- and bush-packed finger that pokes out into Lake Michigan. Over 300 species of birds have been spotted on this unofficial Chicago landing pad for our feathered friends. Located along a natural migratory corridor, this phenomenal hedge almost magically attracts birds as the first natural cover that southbound migrant birds hit after flying the 307-mile length of Lake Michigan. But it likely earned its nickname from the many human visitors that enjoy toking on other mystifying herbs among the peaceful, secluded greenery.

In the spring and fall, the Magic Hedge bustles with avian activity, as migrating birds stop to refuel at this natural reserve. Early in the morning, when the rising sun awakens the insects, you will find plenty of birds on the prowl at the breakfast buffet. Take a walk out on the nearby pier, where loons and long-tailed ducks like to linger. In the wintertime, scan the snow-blanketed sand for the elusive and beautiful snowy owls that have been making more frequent Magic Hedge appearances in the past few years. Keep your eyes on the skies, and you just might spot a swooping peregrine falcon.

The Magic Hedge can be found by following Montrose Avenue east, crossing Lake Shore Drive and making your way towards Lincoln Park's lakefront. Take a right at the street next to the bait shop. Follow the curve until you spot the ornithophiles' paradise on your left.

Address 4400 N Simonds Avenue, Chicago, IL 60613 | Getting there Train to Lawrence (Red Line), then CTA bus 81 to Marine Drive & Wilson | Hours Unrestricted | Tip Cricket Hill, located just west of the Magic Hedge, is a popular site for kite flying, thanks to its tree-free gentle slope. Every May, kids step out into the sunshine and harness Chicago's wind power at the hill's Kids & Kites Festival (www.chicagokite.com), an annual tradition established by former mayor and kite enthusiast Richard M. Daley.

54 Magic Inc.

Supplier to magicians and mentalists

Professional smoking thumbs, double-backed decks of Bicycle cards, comprehensive guides to mind control, helix devil sticks, French arm choppers, Insta-snakes, squirting lapel roses – you'll find every trick of the magic trade at Magic Inc., a storied Chicago shop stocked with every prop and put-on you can imagine. This full-service magic shop, where the staff members are all magicians, supplies professional magicians and mentalists. It also doubles as an academy for magicians in training.

From the late 19th century to the Roaring Twenties, Chicago brimmed with magicians. Most came to the rapidly growing city to make their magical marks at the 1893 World's Columbian Exposition, then stayed to perform in vaudeville theaters, shops, and taverns, and even on street corners.

Famed Chicago magician Laurie L. Ireland, best known for pulling incredible objects out of his jacket sleeves, opened his L. L. Ireland Magic Co. in 1926, when Chicago was already an established magic epicenter. Later he married fellow magician Frances Ahrens Vandevier, founder of the Magigals, a society of lady magicians. Laurie died in 1954, and Frances took over the shop, later marrying Jay Marshall, a noted ventriloquist. They moved the shop to a new location and renamed it Magic Inc. The shop remains in the family today. Jay Marshall's son Alexander "Sandy" Marshall, a theatrical producer living in New York City and two-time Emmy Award winner, splits his time between NYC and Chicago to maintain the family magic business.

If you're considering a career change, take a class – for new as well as experienced magicians. A small theater in the rear of the shop gives budding magicians the chance to test new acts onstage. Magic manuals galore will guide you through literally every trick in the book, while shop staff are happy to demo tools and tricks of the trade.

Address 1838 W Lawrence Avenue, Chicago, IL 60640, +1 (773) 334-2855, www.magicinc.net | Getting there Train to Damen (Brown Line) | Hours Mon–Thu noon–6pm, Fri noon–7pm, Sat 10:30am–5:30pm, Sun noon–5pm | Tip Third-generation Chicago magician extraordinaire Dennis Watkins performs an intimate evening of classic magic on Friday and Saturday evenings at his Magic Parlor in Chicago's historic Palmer House Hotel. Advance reservations are required, at www.themagicparlourchicago.com.

55 Malliway Bros. Magic & Witchcraft

Manifest your intentions

Modern-day witchcraft has seen a resurgence in recent years. Wiccans cast spells by setting up a personal, sacred space, setting clear intentions, and invoking unseen forces, a process that emphasizes positive intentions and harm to none.

Brothers Wycke and Blake Malliway have dedicated their lives to the study and practice of witchcraft. Their Roger's Park Malliway Bros. Magic & Witchcraft shop is a treasure trove of magical supplies, offering everything you need to make magic happen, including a selection of 100+ ritual herbs, oils, incense, and cauldron spirits, all meticulously crafted in small batches and charged by the shop's witches, ensuring their potency and effectiveness at invoking the power of specific deities or spirits.

This is the go-to shop for anyone in need of a "break up," "fast luck," or "attract love" candle, for anyone looking to secure some dragon's blood sage to boost the passion factor in your life, or crushed oyster shell to purify your soul, or even horehound, a perennial herb from the mint family, known for its oval-shaped leaves and tiny white flowers to increase mojo. In-shop experts will help you determine which act of magic may best suit your current spiritual needs.

What truly sets Malliway Bros. apart is their commitment to fostering a sense of community and spiritual growth. If you yearn to start practicing the craft or have been looking for ways to build upon your existing practices, consider taking one of the Malliway brothers' in-store workshops, which incorporate hands-on and interactive components. They also host regular events, such as full moon rituals, where participants can gather to perform spells, or meet-ups where local witches and warlocks can bond over their shared interest in the mystical arts.

Address 1407 W Morse Avenue, Chicago, IL 60626, +1 (773) 754-7546, www.malliwaybros.com, info@malliwaybros.com | Getting there Train to Morse (Red Line) | Hours Mon–Fri noon–8pm, Sat & Sun 11am–8pm | Tip During spring, summer, and fall, the Malliway brothers host 'Witches Conclaves' outdoors, in the forests surrounding Chicago, where it's easier to reconnect with the raw, spiritual energy of nature. Register at malliwaybros.com/witches-conclave.

56 McCormick Bridgehouse

Step inside an iconic Chicago bridge

If you are lucky, you might catch the spectacle that takes place, like clockwork, twice a year: in spring, the glorious, moveable bridges of Chicago are raised, one by one, in synchronized succession, from the south to the north and finally to the east, as boats come happily out of storage and head to their Lake Michigan harbors for boating season. In the fall, the iconic bridges open gradually once again, serenading the boats back to dry storage for the winter. If you happen to be walking across a Chicago bridge when the lifting signal sounds, just make sure to run as fast as you can to the other side.

Chicago has more movable bridges than any other city in the world. In downtown Chicago alone, there are 20 movable bridges, which open over 30,000 times throughout the year as more than 50,000 boats travel smoothly down the river. It takes about eight minutes to raise and lower a Chicago-style drawbridge.

Part of the revolutionary 1920 double-decker Michigan Avenue (now DuSable) Bridge, the McCormick Bridgehouse and Chicago River Museum gives visitors the chance to step inside an iconic Chicago moveable bridge and watch firsthand as all the large and small gears work elegantly in sync to lift up and let multiple boats pass through. Located on the south end of Michigan Avenue, the 1,400-square-foot museum begins at river level and spirals five stories up. Educational exhibits showcase the history of the river as well as the science and technology behind the lifting bridges spectacle. Climb to the top of the Bridgehouse, where a splendid 360-degree view of both the city and river awaits.

The Bridgehouse is seasonal and open May through October. You will need to make a special reservation to take part in the twice annual lifting of the bridges. Be sure to check the museum's schedule of bridge lifts at bridgehousemuseum.org/bridge-lifts and order tickets in advance.

Address 99 Chicago Riverwalk, Chicago, IL 60601, +1 (312) 977-0227, www.bridgehousemuseum.org | Getting there Train to State / Lake (Brown, Orange, Purple, Green, and Pink Line) | Hours Daily May – Oct; see website for seasonal hours | Tip Chicago's one and only fish hotel is located in the river, beside the McCormick Bridgehouse Hotel. The hotel is actually a floating garden that provides rest and a safe harbor for sunfish, bluegills, carp and other finned friends that pass through the big city to spend the night. See how many fish you can spot mingling in the hotel's seaweed-filled lobby (www.chicagoriver.org/about-us/success-stories/fish-hotel).

57 Merz Apothecary

Dreamy drugstore

Peter Merz, a Chicago pharmacist of Swiss descent, was riding the rising tide of the retail drug industry when he opened his Lincoln Square apothecary in 1875. Catering to new immigrants, Merz was fluent in several languages and fond of concocting Old World remedies, making Merz a go-to place for unconventional medical advice with a side of neighborhood gossip. "We still have a recipe book that has handwritten formulations dating back more than 100 years," shares current Merz owner, Anthony Qaiyum. "This was from the days when doctors would write up a prescription that then had to be compounded by hand."

Peer inside the leaded glass windows and you'll spot all the hallmarks of a classic apothecary from days gone by: tin ceilings, solid oak cabinets stocked with antique pharmacy jars and herb containers, and comfy leather chairs. The elegant wooden shelves are stocked with over 13,000 herbal tea remedies, natural supplements, a huge selection of hard-to-find European body and bath products, essential-oil-based perfumes, traditional shaving equipment, beard-care products and more, plus a well-trained staff eager to match you with the products that will work best for you. Merz also carries the largest collection of natural and luxury soaps from around the world under one roof.

The store remained in the Merz family for 85 years until 1972, when the last of the Merz', Ralph, handed the business over to Abdul Qaiyum, a 26-year-old Indian-born pharmacist. Qaiyum's son Anthony has now filled his dad's shoes, earning the respect of yet another generation of customers.

The staff today collectively speaks seven languages, and just like yesteryear, dishes out alternative medical and unscripted life advice to a new clientele, including newly-arrived immigrants looking for familiar, natural remedies that you can't find at your standard retail drugstore.

Address 4716 N Lincoln Avenue, Chicago, IL 60625, +1 (773) 989-0900, www.merzapothecary.com | Getting there Train to Western (Brown Line) | Hours Daily 10am–6pm | Tip Lincoln Square's DANK Haus German American Cultural Center is a cultural hub for German Americans in Chicago, thanks to a wide array of events. The popular Stammtisch Open Haus is a social evening for people who have a mutual interest in German Chicago, held the third Friday of every month, and German Cinema Now offers a chance to view current films from German-speaking countries (with English subtitles) the fourth Friday of each month (4740 N Western Avenue, +1 (773) 561-9181, www.dankhaus.com).

58 Midway Park Plane Spotting

Watching for wings overhead

Built on a 320-acre plot in 1927, Chicago Municipal Airport, later named Midway International Airport, is one of the oldest airports in the country. By the 1930s, it was also one of the world's busiest airports. Throughout its history, Midway has been a significant hub for both passenger and airmail services, playing a crucial role in the development of commercial aviation in the US, though it lost its status as the city's main airport with the opening of O'Hare Airport in 1955. Currently, about 229 flights take off from its runways every day.

Midway Airport's airfield is designed as a square surrounded by four main roads. Tall, white walls separate the planes from the cars, and bright blue signs greet visitors at two corners. If you're driving nearby, you'll likely see planes flying overhead. However, there's one spot with particularly amazing views. At the corner of West 63rd Street and Cicero Avenue, near the southeast corner of the airport, there's a small park with paved pathways and beautiful gardens. The park's walkways even mimic Midway's famous criss-crossing runways.

The busiest times at Midway International Airport are typically during the early morning and late afternoon to early evening. Evening visits to this spot are especially magical, and those in the know say that twilight is the best time to go. Bring a blanket or lawn chairs, grab a deep dish pizza to-go from Giordano's across the street, and then sit back, relax, and watch airplanes take off into the clouds.

Midway Airport was renamed in 1949 to honor the Battle of Midway, a pivotal naval battle in the Pacific during World War II. While you're at the airport, check out the Battle of Midway Exhibit in Concourse A for a fascinating look at the history behind the airport's name, including a multi-media display and a Douglas SBD Dauntless dive bomber suspended from the ceiling.

Address Southeast corner of West 63rd Street and Cicero Avenue, Chicago, IL 60638 | Getting there CTA bus 54B, 63, 63W, 165, 379 to Cicero & 63rd | Hours Unrestricted | Tip During your next trip, Midway Airport's yoga room, located in Concourse C, offers a quiet retreat with exercise mats, natural light, plants, and a spot to store your luggage (West Balmoral Avenue, www.flychicago.com/midway/ServicesAmenities/amenities/Pages/yoga.aspx).

59 Montrose Saloon
The last of the corner bars

In the early 1900s, Chicago boasted over 8,000 saloons, many of which were located on street corners. These bars were more than just places to drink; they were social centers where immigrants could find a sense of belonging, make friends, and even secure jobs. Each neighborhood bar often catered to the predominant ethnic group in its area, providing a familiar environment for new arrivals who didn't yet speak English. The ease of obtaining liquor licenses and the support from breweries, which provided everything from alcohol to glassware, made it relatively simple to open a tavern.

However, the landscape of Chicago's corner bars began to change with the rise of the temperance movement and Prohibition in the 1920s. Post-prohibition, the number of neighborhood bars gradually declined due to shifting demographics, changing attitudes towards public drinking, and urban development. Despite these changes, the legacy of these corner bars lives on in the few that remain.

Montrose Saloon in Albany Park has been a local favorite for decades. Nestled at the base of an old, two-story building at Richmond and Montrose, this unassuming spot is known for its warm atmosphere, cheap beer, and live bluegrass music, a genre with roots in Chicago that can be traced back to the 1930s when Bill Monroe, the "Father of Bluegrass," moved to the city and performed on WLS's "National Barn Dance," one of the most influential radio programs of the time.

The bar's interior features a charmingly worn wooden bar, vintage décor, and a unique "Trading Post," where patrons can swap books, CDs, and other items. Montrose Saloon stands out as a genuine, character-filled spot amidst the city's ever-changing bar scene. Spend some time here in the cozy beer garden, which was a community effort by the bar's patrons, who helped pour the cement after the saloon owner's husband passed away.

Address 2933 W Montrose Avenue, Chicago, IL 60618, +1 (773) 463 7663, www.facebook.com/montrosesaloon | Getting there CTA bus 78 to Montrose & Sacramento | Hours Mon–Wed 4pm–midnight, Thu 4pm–2am, Fri & Sat 1pm–2am, Sun 1pm–midnight | Tip Enjoy live music, including bluegrass, jazz, and open mic, every night of the week at the Gallery Cabaret, a Bucktown neighborhood institution that features local musicians (2020 N Oakley Avenue, www.gallerycabaret.com).

60 Morgan Shoal and Shipwreck

Chicago's sunken treasure

Three hundred feet off the South Side Chicago shoreline at a depth of about twenty feet, a submerged Atlantis teems with life. The 32-acre Morgan Shoal, a limestone shelf unearthed when glaciers gouged the basin of Lake Michigan centuries ago, represents one of the most biodiverse ecologies in the Midwest, confirmed by studies conducted by the nearby Shedd Aquarium. Quagga mussels grip the shoal, while gobies, lake trout, largemouth bass, yellow perch, and the rare isopods – which first made their appearance on our planet during the Paleozoic Era, some 300 million years ago – find their way through the algae-coated nooks and crannies of Chicago's take on the coral reef.

Snorkel out to this underwater ecology, and you won't believe you are in Chicago. On a clear, calm day, visibility can reach about 20 feet, making it easy to spot the many creatures swimming the shallow shoal. Peep your head above the water to break your tropical reverie and take a look at the Chicago skyline that stands in the distance.

Immediately southwest of the Morgan Shoal lie the remains of the Silver Spray, an 1894 excursion ship. In July of 1914, the 109-foot passenger boat was carrying a group of University of Chicago students on their way to tour the steel mills of Northwest Indiana, when it hit the rocky Morgan Shoal and sank. Most of the 109-foot boat was recovered and burned ashore in bonfires, but the boiler and propeller remain in place. When the lake's water levels are low, the boiler of the Silver Spray, often mistaken for a boulder from the shoreline, pokes up out of the water.

It is an easy swim from Morgan Point out to this unofficial wildlife reserve. A mask, snorkel, and fins will make your trip easier, as will a wet suit, because lake water temperatures are decidedly non-tropical.

Address Lake Michigan, 300 feet off Morgan Point at E 47th Street and S Lake Shore Drive | Getting there Train to 47th Street Kenwood (Metra Electric Line) | Tip Underwater Safaris rents snorkeling gear and can also arrange for private, guided dives of Morgan Shoal as well as other Lake Michigan wrecks (2950 N Lincoln Avenue, +1 (773) 348-3999, www.uwsafaris.com).

61 Murder Castle Site

Check out any time you like, but you can never leave

H. H. Holmes was the first documented serial killer in US history. An itinerant grifter and bigamist, he arrived in Chicago in 1883 with murder on his mind.

By 1892 he had secretly constructed a complex Murder Castle that masqueraded as a World's Fair hotel. Though the building was mysteriously gutted by fire in 1895 and replaced in 1939 by the US post office that still stands on the site, many find the area charged with paranormal activity to this day. Nine murders were confirmed during investigations, but it is estimated that over 200 unlucky guests checked in to Holmes' World Fair hotel and never checked out… alive.

Holmes designed his building as a fully-operating murder machine. Though he wasn't a trained architect, he came up with a plan for a three-story home at the corner of 63rd Street and S Wallace Avenue that called for dozens of rooms, hidden chambers, dissection facilities, trap doors, dumbwaiters, a gas chamber, secret stairways, and passages, as well as an elaborate alarm system. The basement contained a complete crematory, with vats for body disposal via quicklime ready to greet the unluckiest of hotel guests.

By constantly hiring and firing construction workers, he was able to keep his macabre vision hidden from the public. His timing was well planned, too: Holmes' Murder Castle was ready for business in 1892, so he could easily find unwitting lodgers looking for housing while attending the nearby World's Columbian Exposition.

On May 7, 1896, Holmes was hanged. Shortly before his death he himself remarked that he had taken on "a satanical cast." Rumors persist about the location being haunted by the boarders that never emerged. Neighbors claim that dogs will cross the street rather than walk adjacent to the building, while others report hearing the ghastly screams of Holmes' torture victims in the dead of night.

Address 63rd Street and S Wallace Avenue, Chicago, IL 60621 | Getting there Train to Halsted (Green, Red Line or Metra BNSF Railway Line) | Hours Unrestricted from the outside | Tip Erik Larson's bestselling nonfiction book, *The Devil in the White City*, chronicles Holmes' murderous mindset.

62 Neon Shop Fishtail
Timeless glow

Since its discovery in 1898 and its first appearance in the US in 1923 at a Packard Auto Dealership, neon has been a glowing part of American life. While Chicago was once alight with neon, every year, more of the city's iconic neon signs go dark. The use of neon signage peaked from 1920 to 1960, but since then, it has been on a steady decline due to easily breakable glass tubes, high energy costs, and difficulty finding someone to maintain this unique form of light.

Enter Neon Shop Fishtail, a Chicago store that specializes in custom and vintage neon and emphasizes restoring classic, old neon signs. Owner Tom Brickler entered the world of neon when his beloved Budweiser beer sign broke, and he couldn't find a place that would repair it. Brickler named his store Neon Shop Fishtail after the fishtail-shaped ribbon burner used to create big, wide, sweeping bends in glass tubes. "Also, I went into business in the '80s," laughs Brickler, "and it was either going to sink or swim."

"Neon light" is the term for light from gas contained in a delicate, glass tube. When high voltage is applied to the electrodes at each end of the tube, the gas inside becomes ionized and emits a bright, colorful light. The color of the light depends on the gas inside the tube. For example, neon gas produces red light, helium produces yellow or pink light, and mercury produces blue light.

Brickler's showroom and repair shop are packed with over 1,000 new and vintage neon signs, making the venue more of a museum than a shop. You might recognize some signs from old Chicago motels, restaurants, and car repair shops that are no longer in business. Ask to see the most prized vintage sign in Tom's collection: a neon and porcelain chicken keeping her eggs warm in a basket. Bring in your neon dream, and Brickler and his team will work with you to make it glow into a customized neon sign of your own.

Address 2247 N Western Avenue, Chicago, IL 60647, +1 (773) 227-0303, www.neonshopfishtail.com, neoneon@gmail.com | Getting there Train to California or Western (Blue Line) | Hours Mon–Fri 8:30am–4:30pm, Sat 10am–1pm and by appointment | Tip Neon Shop Fishtail's beautiful store operated as a women's bathhouse in the roaring 20s. See if you can spot the lovely terra-cotta motif of a naked lady sailing on a slice of the moon on the building's façade (2247 N Western Avenue).

63 Obama's Barber Chair

Presidential trims

Before he became the 44th president of the United States, Barack Obama was just an average Chicagoan, living with his beautiful wife and two daughters in a lovely Georgian revival mansion at 5046 S Greenwood Avenue. He tucked into scrambled eggs, hash browns, and sausage at Valois Cafeteria (1518 E 53rd Street), browsed the dusty shelves of 57th Street Books (1301 E 57th Street), and had his hair cut at the humble Hyde Park Hair Salon.

Since 1927, the salon has catered to men looking for a quality shave and a haircut. Spike Lee, Phil Gates, Devon Hester, Bill Veeck, Suge Knight, and former Chicago mayor Harold Washington were all regulars, and Obama was a loyal patron of more than 17 years. While serving as our nation's president, Obama continued to have his hair cut by the salon's owner Ishmael Coye so he could keep up with his favorite barber.

Today, visitors to the storied salon can sit beside the exact chair Barack Obama sat in while receiving his trims. Friendly service and sage advice are a given at this old-school-style barbershop that doubles as a makeshift shrine to the Chicago Bears, boxing legend Muhammad Ali, who also used to live in the neighborhood, and of course, hometown hero, Obama. The salon is a full-service shop that also offers manicures, pedicures, hot lather shaves, facials, massage therapy and shoe shines. Even bald men can count on a stellar service that will leave their head polished and protected. The $21 Obama Cut promises you'll leave the salon as dapper as the former president. Walk-ins are welcome, but your best bet is to call ahead for an appointment.

Unfortunately, visitors hoping to sit in the chair will be disappointed. In February 2009, R. S. Owens & Company, the Chicago-based manufacturer of trophies, including the Academy Awards, gifted the salon a Plexiglas case to protect this piece of presidential history.

Address Dorchester Commons Shopping Center, 5234 S Blackstone Avenue, Chicago, IL 60615, +1 (773) 493-6028, www.hydeparkhairsalon.com | **Getting there** Train to 55th-56th-57th Street (Metra Electric and South Shore Line) | **Hours** Daily 9am – 8pm | **Tip** A simple rock with a metallic plate at 53rd Street and S Dorchester in Hyde Park marks the spot where former President Barack Obama first kissed his wife Michelle. This was once the site of a Baskin-Robbins ice cream shop, where the young couple enjoyed a moment sweeter than a sundae on their very first date back in the summer of 1989.

64 — Old St. Patrick's Church

Cornerstone of Irish culture

Founded by faithful Irish immigrants on Easter Sunday, 1846, in a wooden building at Randolph Street and Desplaines Street, vibrant Old St. Patrick's Church is considered the cornerstone of Irish-American culture in Chicago. The present Romanesque-style church building, with its glorious Celtic Revival ornamentation, soaring octagonal spire, and yellow Cream City brick from Milwaukee set on a Lemont limestone base, was dedicated on Christmas Day, 1856, making it one of the few buildings to survive the Chicago Fire and the oldest standing church building in the city of Chicago. Celebrate mass here to connect with seven generations of parishioners, take part in one of the church's many neighborhood, volunteer outreach programs, or attend the summer block party, where chances are good that you will probably bump into your future bride or groom.

St. Patrick's been connecting faith, community, and the Irish culture in Chicago, which boasts the fourth-largest population of Irish Americans in the country, for close to 175 years. Upon arrival in Chicago, Irish immigrants would head straight to St. Pat's where they were welcomed with food, shelter, and the support of other parishioners who were already well on their way towards the American Dream.

The interior of the church, which many compare to sitting inside an Easter egg, was inspired by the Celtic art exhibit at the Columbian Exposition of 1893. Chicago artist Thomas O'Shaughnessy created the 15 magnificent, Art Nouveau stained-glass windows, each pane inspired by the Book of Kells and depicting a scene from the lives of the famous saints of Ireland. A towering statue of St. Patrick stands by the altar, welcoming his Irish family to Chicago.

In 1997, Oprah Winfrey deemed it one of the best places to meet your future spouse, and the event has led to 105 confirmed marriages.

Address 700 W Adams Street, Chicago, IL 60661, +1 (312) 648-1021, www.oldstpats.org, info@oldstpats.org | Getting there Train to Clinton (Blue Line) | Hours Daily 7am–1pm; see website for services and events | Tip Docents are available to conduct guided tours of Old St. Pat's between 8 and 11am, Monday through Friday.

65 Optimo Hats
Bringing back bold elegance one hat at a time

Chicago was once a hat-wearing town, with new styles of classic men's hats hitting the streets every decade. Smart hats were de rigueur for the modern man, no matter his profession, social status, or stature. Then came John F. Kennedy, who rarely wore a hat of any kind during his presidency, setting off a trend that brings us to bare-headed today. Optimo Hats is on a mission to bring back bold, elegant statement hats to men in Chicago and beyond.

The walls and display windows of Optimo Hats are lined with the most beautiful men's hats you'll ever encounter. Straw hats are made from the highest quality hand-woven straw, imported from Ecuador, while the felt of the fedoras is crafted from wild animal furs, as opposed to cheaper wool alternatives. The bindings and ribbons are hand-stitched with the finest silk threads.

A retro circumference-measuring tool and a flange stand, used to flatten and shape the brim to each customer's taste, ensure the perfect custom fit. The hats here are offered in three sizes between conventional sizes, as well as in four oval head shapes, creating an individualized, air-cushioned fit. The sales staff will guide you towards that impossibly perfect-fitting hat, which should gently grip your head and yet be able to be easily tugged down a bit when the windy city lives up to its reputation. Prices match the time-consuming hat making process coupled with the finest materials; the most expensive hats run into the thousands. You might recognize Optimo hats in the movies *J. Edgar*, *Public Enemies*, and *Road to Perdition*.

Customers also have their pick from a wide range of fine vintage and modern hat ribbons from around the world. Once the ribbon is traditionally folded and sewn by hand using traditional millinery stitches to craft the bow and ensure no thread is visible, you'll know you're walking away with a museum-quality masterpiece that will bring a little more retro class and style to your modern-day life.

Address 51 W Jackson Boulevard, Chicago, IL 60604, +1 (312) 922-2999, www.optimo.com, info@optimo.com | Getting there Train to Jackson (Blue Line) or Harold Washington Library-State / Van Buren (Brown, Orange, Pink, and Purple Line) | Hours Mon–Sat 11am–5pm | Tip See if you can spot the 31-foot-tall statue of the Roman goddess Ceres who keeps watch from the top of the nearby Chicago Board of Trade. Though it's normally closed to the public, the Chicago Board of Trade offers private tours by appointment (141 W Jackson Boulevard, www.cbot.com).

66 — Osaka Garden
Rising phoenix

Chicago's White City bloomed into being for the 1893 World's Columbian Exposition, dazzling visitors with its grand neoclassical buildings, surrounded by canals and ornate gardens designed by renowned landscape architect Frederick Law Olmsted.

But these opulent structures were not designed to last forever. The fancy façades were made not of marble, but of a cheap mixture of plaster, cement, and jute fiber, whitewashed with oil and lead paint. Of the over 200 buildings erected for the exposition, only two still stand. After the fair was over, Jackson Park, the expo's epicenter, was transformed into an interconnected system of serene lagoons surrounding the 15-acre Wooded Island.

Wooded Island was where fairgoers went to catch a breath of fresh air. At its northern end stood the Ho-o-Den, a.k.a. Phoenix Pavilion, a showcase of Japanese fine arts. At the southern end was the strolling garden, or *kyuushiki,* with its double pond, cascading waterfall, and stone pathways through the cherry blossom trees. Now known as the Osaka Garden and named for the long-standing Sister Cities relationship with the city of Osaka in Japan, the garden's blooming flowers offered welcome shade and respite to fairgoers and modern strollers today.

In the 1930s, more Japanese elements were added, including the scenic Moon Bridge and stone lanterns. Across the lagoon lies the last remaining structure of the 1893 fair, the Palace of Fine Arts, which is today's Museum of Science and Industry.

In 2014, the garden closed so that the US Army Corps of Engineers could step in to restore the eroding lagoon shores, reset rocks, and replace invasive trees with 400,000 native plants. In 2016, Yoko Ono unveiled the lotus-inspired Sky Landing, her first permanent work of art in the Americas, as a gesture of peace, harmony and healing in the rebirthed garden.

Address 6401 S South Stony Island Avenue, Chicago, IL 60637, www.hydepark.org | Getting there Train to 63rd Street (Metra Electric Line) | Hours Daily 9am–5pm | Tip The "Golden Lady" sculpture, a one-third scale replica of Daniel Chester French's original Statue of the Republic, which was the centerpiece of the 1893 World's Columbian Exposition, stands in the area between the exposition's Electricity and Administration Buildings (both demolished after the exposition), now an intersection, where Richards Drive joins Hayes Drive (www.hydepark.org).

67 Outspoken at Sidetrack

Everyone has a story

Chicago's Boystown is home to highly active, visible, and vibrant LGBTQ communities. As the first officially recognized gay village in the country, this dynamic East Lakeview neighborhood, bordered by Lake Michigan on the east and Clark Street on the west, Irving Park Road to the north and Diversey Avenue to the south, is home to over 30 different gay and lesbian bars, nightclubs, and restaurants. If you want to find the beating heart of this community, you'll do so at Sidetrack, a huge Boystown hotspot that offers a monthly live storytelling show focused on the personal stories of LGBTQ-identified performers: Outspoken.

The stories told at Outspoken range from the side-splitting to the tear-jerking. Expect six storytellers from all walks of life, sharing stories that are not always gay-themed but always thought-provoking. Intimate and lively, this is a monthly event that aims to create a connection between the storytellers and the audience members, making for a wonderful opportunity to interact with the Boystown community in a fun and friendly atmosphere. Kim Hunt of Affinity Community Services, a social justice organization that focuses on health and wellness, leadership development, and community building among Chicago's LGBTQ youth, and Art Johnston, founder of Equality Illinois, serve as emcees. Each show promises to be unique, and the roster of featured storytellers changes each month. One reviewer calls Outspoken, "One of the best evenings you will spend in the midst of humanity."

Sidetrack, which lies at the heart of Boystown on the Halsted strip, spans more than eight storefronts and multiple levels, including an open-air courtyard and a lush rooftop deck. In addition to Outspoken, the bar hosts a variety of other community-minded fundraisers and events throughout the year. There is no cover fee, but you must be 21 and have a valid ID.

Address Sidetrack, 3349 N Halsted Street, Chicago, IL 60657, +1 (773) 477-9189, www.sidetrackchicago.com | Getting there Train to Belmont (Red, Brown, and Purple Line) | Hours First Tue of every month; doors open 6pm; stories begin 7pm | Tip The city's annual Gay and Lesbian Pride Parade kicks off on the last Sunday of June with marching bands, grand floats, dance troupes, twirlers, celebrities and many political figures parading down Halsted and Broadway, the main streets of Boystown (www.chicagopride.gopride.com).

68 Oz Park

Follow the yellow brick road

In the 1890s, a certain L. Frank Baum, a reporter for the *Chicago Evening Post*, dreamed up a fantastical story: a cyclone whirls a young farm girl and her little dog up and away and into a land inhabited by merry Munchkins, winged monkeys, a wicked witch, and a charlatan ruler. Though the name Oz came from his file cabinet labeled "O-Z," many scholars of this American fairy tale believe that the mystical land was inspired by the glimmering "White City" that was the 1893 Chicago World's Fair.

Baum's beloved characters, who jumped from the printed page to the silver screen in 1939, live on in charming Oz Park. From the corner of Webster Avenue and Larabee Street, follow the yellow brick road towards the Emerald Garden, where you will be greeted by the Scarecrow. At the southeast corner, the bronze Cowardly Lion proudly displays his badge of courage. Dorothy and Toto watch over the children as they head towards the playground swings and slides. The Tin Man guards the northeast corner, proudly displaying his brand new, ticking heart. The statues were all created by John Kearney, a Chicago and Provincetown-based artist famous for his figurative sculptures made of found metal objects. He welded together old chrome car bumpers to bring Oz Park's Tin Man to life.

One of the park's major benefactors shares a first name with the Kansas girl who lost and then found herself in the Land of Oz: Dorothy Melamerson, a Chicago public school physical education teacher, who preferred to live a frugal life so that she could ultimately gift the children of her city this cherished, 13-plus-acre park. Melamerson also donated enough money to create the park's baseball fields and basketball, tennis, and volleyball courts, as well as the extensive youth sports initiative, a legacy that is reflected in the smiling faces of the many youngsters who joyfully claim this park as their own.

Address 2021 N Burling Street, Chicago, IL 60614, www.chicagoparkdistrict.com/parks | Getting there Train to Armitage (Brown and Purple Line) | Hours Daily dawn–dusk | Tip Oz Park is one of many Chicago parks that show free outdoor movies as part of the "Movies in the Park" summer series. Bring a blanket and spread it on the grass, under the stars, for a truly unique movie-going experience (www.chicagoparkdistrict.com/events/movies).

69 — Palm Court at the Drake Hotel

Timeless tea

For nearly a century, savvy ladies have spent entire afternoons sipping tea beside a fountain in the Drake Hotel's gilded Palm Court. No one can pinpoint exactly why time stands still in this posh retreat as you enjoy your elegant afternoon tea. Maybe it is the enchanting ambiance amidst an array of potted palms, coupled with the pre-tea coupe of champagne. Perhaps it is the soft, flattering light emanating from the stained-glass ceiling and the lulling melodies of the live harpist. Queen Elizabeth, Princess Diana, and the Empress of Japan have all luxuriated in a spot of tea at the timeless Palm Court.

Every day afternoon tea is served between 1pm and 5pm at the Palm Court, located just off the hotel's main lobby. Seventeen tea selections created by Le Palais des Thés are on the menu, including the original Palm Court blend, all served in signature sterling silver teapots. Tiered platters of finger sandwiches, festive petit fours, English scones, and mini lemon poppyseed loaves are accompanied by fine preserves, lemon curd, and rich English Devon Cream.

The centerpiece of the Palm Court is the gorgeous marble fountain overflowing with flowers. Don't leave without making a wish, as the fountain is filled with coins that are donated to a local charity after a year's worth of accumulation.

Chicago's Drake Hotel has been welcoming visitors from its perch at the start of the Magnificent Mile since it was inaugurated on New Year's Eve in 1920. Designed with the palaces of High Renaissance Italy in mind, the hotel's 537 guest rooms and 74 suites have hosted important cultural and political figures from around the world. Several movies have been filmed under its roof, including *Time and Again* (1980), *The Blues Brothers* (1980), *Continental Divide* (1981), *Risky Business* (1983), and *My Best Friend's Wedding* (1997).

Address 140 E Walton Place, Chicago, IL 60611, +1 (312) 787-2200, www.thedrakehotel.com/dining/palm-court | Getting there Train to Chicago (Red Line) | Hours See website for seasonal hours and tea services | Tip Post-tea, head to the bar at the Drake's Coq d'Or for bookbinder soup (a Drake classic) and executive martinis.

70 Palmer Mausoleum

Beware of wandering ghosts

Potter Palmer and his stunning wife Bertha were the toast of Gilded Age Chicago. Potter is best known for developing State Street, and in particular for his enormous Palmer House Hotel, a wedding gift that literally went up in flames. He built the elegant hotel, the first of its kind in Chicago, in honor of his beautiful new wife, Bertha. An unlucky thirteen days after his hotel opened on September 26, 1871, it burned down to the ground in the Great Chicago Fire.

But not even the Great Chicago Fire could derail the Palmers' dreams. Potter secured a $1.7 million signature loan and rebuilt his hotel and his fortune. Bertha, who Potter so famously spoiled with diamonds and pearls, went to become the queen of Chicago high society, a patron of Impressionist artists and the inventor of the brownie.

While the Palmers lived in a Gold Coast Gothic-style castle, today they rest eternally within the two large granite sarcophagi at ghostly Graceland Cemetery. Three generations of their descendants lie beside them in this, the grandest tomb of Graceland. It was designed by the firm of McKim, Mead & White to resemble a Greek temple. When Mrs. Palmer died in Florida in 1918, she was transported here in a coffin covered in a blanket of orchids. The inverted torches on the sides of their sarcophagi symbolize death.

The Victorian Graceland Cemetery is considered to be one of the most paranormally active sites in Chicago, so beware of wandering ghosts. It is the final resting place of many of Chicago's most illustrious early citizens. Architect Louis Sullivan, who is also buried here, designed the ornate tomb of lumber baron Henry Harrison Getty. An Egyptian-style granite pyramid serves as the mausoleum for the family of beer brewer Peter Schoenhofen. Industrialist George Pullman rests here in a steel-and-concrete reinforced vault, to prevent his body from being exhumed by angry labor activists.

POTTER PALMER
MDCCCXXVI
MCMII

Address 4001 N Clark Street, Chicago, IL 60613, +1 (773) 525-1105, www.gracelandcemetery.org | Getting there Train to Sheridan (Red Line) | Hours Wed, Fri & Sat 11am–5pm, Thu 11am–6pm | Tip A spooky statue by famous American sculptor Lorado Taft marks the grave of early Chicago pioneer Dexter Graves (1789–1844). The mysterious, bronze hooded man was officially named Eternal Silence. It is more commonly referred to as the Statue of Death. Legend has it that if you look into the statue's black eyes, you will see your own death unfold.

71 Palmisano Park

From coral reef to quarry to peaceful city oasis

Palmisano Park knows a thing or two about adapting to the changing tides of time. Over the centuries, it has transformed from a coral reef to a quarry, to landfill, and finally to the beautiful 27-acre park that it is today. Located in the heart of Bridgeport, this peaceful park, with its fishing pond, wetlands, quarry walls, and trailways, is one of Chicago's most dynamic green spaces.

Once upon a time – 400 million years ago to be exact – this green escape from the city was part of a massive coral reef in the warm, shallow seas that covered what is now Chicago. As the Silurian Age faded into history, Dolomite limestone and fossils formed as curious ancient souvenirs. Later, in the late 1830s, when early entrepreneurs turned the site into a quarry, that same limestone was mined and used to build railroad embankments, bridges, tunnels, lake retaining walls, homes, foundations, and façades throughout Chicago. The quarry continued operating until 1970, its excavated hole having reached 380 feet below street level, when it was turned into a landfill for clean construction debris.

In 1999, the city decided to transform the park into much-needed green space, and in 2009, Palmisano Park was inaugurated. It has been hailed as one of the best places to enjoy spending time outdoors, no matter the season.

Walk along over 1.7 miles of paths, where you are sure to find signs of Palmisano Park's past, such as the catch-and-release fishing pond situated 40 feet below street level which retains the original walls of the old quarry. Reclaimed wood found in the quarry was used to create the walkways. Old rocks from the quarry days dot the landscape. Climb the hill, which rises 33 feet above street level, to see the quarry's limestone legacy, a stunning view of the city built with the remains of an ancient reef mined from this now verdant corner of Bridgeport.

Address 2700 S Halsted Street, Chicago, IL 60608, +1 (312) 747-6497, www.chicagoparkdistrict.com/parks | Getting there Train to Halsted (Orange Line) | Hours Daily dawn–dusk | Tip You can find a free self-guided audio tour of Palmisano Park, created by the Chicago Park District online. The tour includes a map with stopping points that correspond with the audio tracks. If you visit each place and listen to the tracks, your walking tour will take approximately 40 minutes (www.chicagoparkdistrict.com/about-us/audio-tours/palmisano-park).

72 Patio at Salt Shed Pub

Soak in the sounds and Goose Island sips

Originally a natural island home to flocks of geese, Goose Island became a bustling industrial zone for tanneries, soap factories, and breweries in the mid-19th century. Known as "Little Hell" due to the smoke and stench from nearby factories, the tiny island was a melting pot of Irish, Polish, and German immigrants, who balanced urban factory work with rural traditions, like raising livestock.

The island inspired the name of the famous Goose Island Brewery, which started as a small brewpub in 1988 and is now known worldwide for its innovative beers. The patio at Goose Island Brewery's Salt Shed Pub is a fantastic spot to enjoy their craft beers. You also can soak in the sounds of outdoor concerts playing at the adjacent Salt Shed.

The Salt Shed, located at the old Morton Salt facility, is now a vibrant music and event venue that also has a rich history rooted in Chicago's industrial past. Originally built in the 1920s, it served as a key facility for the skeleton-framed Morton Salt Company, where salt was processed, packaged, and distributed. The iconic "Umbrella Girl" sign on the rooftop became a landmark visible from the Kennedy Expressway. In 2015, Morton Salt relocated, and in 2022, the building was transformed into The Salt Shed, a multi-purpose creative hub.

Plan your visit to the patio to coincide with the concert of your choice by checking the Salt Shed's calendar before you go at www.saltshedchicago.com. Try their rotating selection of innovative beers, including some exclusive brews you won't find anywhere else, such as Goose Island's Bourbon County Brand Stout, an imperial stout aged in bourbon barrels and known for its deep, rich flavors of chocolate and vanilla. The brewery often hosts local food trucks, so you can pair your beer with delicious eats. The patio is dog-friendly, making it a perfect spot to bring your furry friend on a fun date.

Address 1221 W Blackhawk Street, Chicago, IL 60642, +1 (312) 312-915-0071, www.gooseisland.com/saltshedpub | Getting there CTA bus 70 to Division & Elston | Hours Wed–Thu noon–10pm, Fri noon–midnight, Sat 10am–midnight, Sun 10am–10pm | Tip Goose Island Beer Company offers tours of their Fulton Avenue brewery (1800 W Fulton Street, www.gooseisland.com/visit). Learn about the brewing process, sample some of their unique beers, and even chat with the brewers.

73 Paul Sereno's Fossil Lab
A paleontologist's wonderland

Paul Sereno's Fossil Lab at the University of Chicago is a treasure trove for paleontology enthusiasts. Located in the Washington Park neighborhood, arguably the most famous paleontologist in the US designed his 6,000-square-foot facility to bring the prehistoric world to life and inspire kids to find their passion and embrace adventure. Skeletons of modern birds, mammals, and alligators hang from the ceilings and line the shelves of this "bone makerspace."

"I see paleontology as an adventure with a purpose," said Sereno in his official University of Chicago bio. "How else to describe a scientific discipline that allows you to romp in remote corners of the globe, resurrecting gargantuan creatures that have never been seen? The trick to big fossil finds? You've got to be able to go where no one has gone before—while learning to enjoy 125°F heat."

Sereno led countless expeditions and discovered several new dinosaur species before co-founding Project Exploration, a nonprofit that aims to make science accessible to the public and inspire young minds. Among the many fascinating objects in this captivating lab are two of Sereno's most famous discoveries: the skull of *Sarcosuchus imperator*, also known as "SuperCroc," a 40-foot-long, prehistoric crocodile, and the bones of Suchomimus, a fish-eating dinosaur that lived between 125 and 112 million years ago during the Early Cretaceous period in what is now Niger in northern Africa.

This is the only place in the US where you can stare into the eye sockets of a *Tyrannosaurus rex* skull, touch the claws of a *Raptorex kriegsteini*, a Tyrannosaurid dinosaur that roamed our planet during the Late Cretaceous period, around 70 million years ago. But perhaps the coolest part of this lab is its glass walls that allow visitors to observe the meticulous work of fossil technicians, sometimes including Sereno himself.

Address 5437 S Wabash Avenue, Chicago, IL 60615, +1 (773) 702-1234, paulsereno.uchicago.edu/fossil_lab | Getting there Train to Garfield (Green Line) | Hours Second Thu of every month 3:30–5pm | Tip Once a cutting-edge bakery where Butternut Bread was crafted, the 1914 Schulze Baking Company building (40 E Garfield Boulevard), an Art Deco gem, now stands as a vacant terra cotta and concrete shell. Step inside this raw and empty space in October, during the Chicago Architecture Foundation's annual Open House Chicago weekend (www.openhousechicago.org).

74 — Pickwick Alley

Passageway to Old Chicago

It is easy to miss Pickwick Lane unless you know it is there. Though it is located in the heart of the bustling Loop at 22 E Jackson Boulevard, this nine-foot-wide passageway, dead-ended by a three-story building, might be short in length, but it is long in history. Step onto its cobblestones and travel back in time to the Chicago of days gone by.

The city of Chicago grew up around that small building, still known as the Pickwick Stable, which is actually 19 feet wide, and 19 feet deep. Over 150 years ago, this lane led to an actual stable that was destroyed in the Great Chicago Fire. After the fire, grocer and flour merchant Henry Horner and his wife Fannie Abson purchased the lot, where they built the current two-story building, transforming the space into Colonel Abson's Chop House, a favorite eating establishment for Chicago's biggest *bon vivants*, especially the post-theatre crowd. The Absons later added the building's third floor and made it their home. After the chop house closed in 1900, a number of restaurants came and went in this space, including the Red Path Inn, Robinson's, Pickwick Cafe and 22 East. In the 1970s, the building was almost torn down, but thankfully this little corner of Old Chicago survived.

A small coffee shop with a few seats in the alley now thrives in what was once nothing more than a dead end and a horse stable. Some call it "an urban leftover," as it has remained as it was for decades while the area around it filled with new skyscrapers. The two buildings that flank the lane are the 16-story Gibbons Building and the 19-story landmarked Steger Building, which was originally home to a piano company. At night, with the tiny lights strung overhead, it is not difficult to imagine the comings and goings in Pickwick Lane and the days when horses made up most of Chicago's traffic.

Address 22 E Jackson Boulevard, Chicago, IL 60604 | Getting there Train to Adams/
Wabash (Brown, Orange, Purple, Green, and Pink Line) | Hours Unrestricted | Tip Steps
away from Pickwick Alley, at Jackson Boulevard and Michigan Avenue, was the original
starting point of the fabled Route 66, America's Main Street.

75 Pilsen Murals
Redefining a neighborhood

The murals that adorn just about every space in the Pilsen neighborhood reflect the residents' shared joys, sorrows, political concerns, memories, and Latino culture. What started as a Chicago Urban Art Society initiative, to drive out gang graffiti and brighten this corner of the city, has turned into a thought-provoking art gallery, sharing the stories of the residents via art and transforming the neighborhood into a creative hub.

Artist Francisco Mendoza was commissioned in 1993 to redefine the gateway to Pilsen. Together with a team of 20 young students, he created *Las Mujeres* (located on the exterior of the station on the east side of the entrance), a mosaic that celebrates the bold and beautiful women of Mexico, past and present. In 1998, Mendoza gathered a group of teens once again and packed the entire station with art – every solid surface is covered with a colorful mural expressing the rich Mexican heritage of Pilsen's residents.

At 1401 W 18th Street, the two-story *Declaration of Immigration*, created by artist Salvador Jimenez and a group of young students, poignantly reminds viewers that we are a city and a nation of immigrants. Pilsen has historically been a first-stop neighborhood for immigrants, having first welcomed immigrants from Bohemia and later from Mexico.

The mural *Gulliver En El País De Las Maravillas* (1900 W Cullerton Street) covers the studio home of its artist, Hector Duarte. Inspired by Gulliver's Travels, it depicts Gulliver not as a traveler in a new land, but as a Mexican immigrant struggling to break free from a barbed wire fence. *Increíbles Las Cosas Q' Se Ven* by Jeff Zimmerman pays homage to the sacrifices of past generations for the benefit of the next, and depicts migrants crossing a river, the faces of blue collar workers, and finally, two proud Mexican-American graduates with a bold and true reminder: "Si, se puede" – Yes, you can.

76 Poetry Foundation
The power of poetry

Ruth Lilly, heiress to the Lilly family pharmaceutical fortune, loved reading and writing poetry. For years she submitted her poems to the renowned *Poetry* magazine, unsuccessfully. Nevertheless, Lilly did not let her rejection undermine her support of the famed magazine. In 2002, she donated $100 million to *Poetry*. Part of her bequest was used to build a new home for the Poetry Foundation, marking the first space in Chicago dedicated solely to the art of poetry.

Founded in Chicago in 1912, *Poetry* is one of the world's leading monthly poetry journals in the English-speaking world, having featured the works of Gwendolyn Brooks, T. S. Eliot, Robert Frost, Ezra Pound, Carl Sandburg, Dylan Thomas, and William Carlos Williams. The Poetry Foundation's new River North headquarters, designed by John Ronan Architects, opened in 2011 and houses a public library, gallery, and garden, as well as office space for the Poetry Foundation and magazine.

When Harriet Monroe founded *Poetry* magazine, she began with an image: the Open Door. "May the great poet we are looking for never find it shut, or half-shut, against his ample genius!" Following Monroe's proclamation, to enter the Poetry Foundation, you walk through an opening in the black screen wall rather than any grand, gilded doors. You can also find Harriet Monroe, in a Pointillist rendering, on the wall next to the performance space door.

Inside, an elevated courtyard features a mirrored tribute to Lilly. The Foundation's extensive library, the Midwest's only library dedicated exclusively to poetry, holds over 30,000 volumes and features private listening booths where visitors can listen to audio and video poetry recordings. While you can always stop in for a moment of poetry reading and repose, the Poetry Foundation hosts almost daily readings, workshops, and performances, for poets and lovers of poetry alike.

Address 61 W Superior Street, Chicago, IL 60654, +1 (312) 787-7070, www.poetryfoundation.org | Getting there Train to Chicago (Red Line) | Hours Mon–Fri 11am–4pm | Tip The Poetry Foundation's POETRY mobile app, available on iTunes and Google Play, gives poetry lovers access to hundreds of poems by classic and contemporary poets. Give your phone a shake to discover new poems to fit any mood.

77__Pothole Art
Bumps in the road

It takes a truckload of ingenuity to transform a troubling eyesore into a work of art. Chicago artist Jim Bachor has gone above and beyond. He has taken on the challenge of patching up Chicago's most dastardly potholes and makes mosaics out of them, thus providing a community service for both the city's streets and its artful spirit. His 30-plus pothole art masterpieces are reminders of the power of creativity to transform even the worst lemons into lemonade, making light of the bumps in the road of life by turning them into places of beauty and creativity.

Chicago's wide range of high and low temperatures makes for plenty of potholes. The period from December through April is considered peak pothole season as the snow and cold cause dangerous cavities to erupt inwards on streets across the city. City road crews fixed potholes in their thousands around the city last year, even going so far as to set up a Pothole Tracker that maps potholes patched by the Department of Transportation in the previous seven days, based on corresponding 311 city service delivery requests. But it seems that as soon as one pit is patched up seemingly for good, another one appears steps away, much to the dismay of Chicago drivers.

Bachor's self-proclaimed pothole revitalization initiative dates back to 2013, when he patched up a pothole in front of his home in the Mayfair neighborhood. He has transformed potholes into beautiful and quirky mosaics, modern versions of Roman mosaic floors. You'll come across ice cream cones, creamsicles, daffodils, blue birds. He has also patched potholes with Burberry plaid, red and green Gucci stripes, and Louis Vuitton logos, as well as helpful messages that say both "Pothole" and "This Is Not a Pothole."

An interactive map at www.bachor.com details the exact locations, but it's best to be caught unaware by these ever-evolving installations.

Address See www.bachor.com for an interactive map of Bachor's playful pothole installations | **Getting there** Varies by location | **Hours** Unrestricted | **Tip** Chicago's streets are arranged in an iconic grid system, the epicenter of which is the intersection of State and Madison Streets, in the heart of the Loop. Each street is prefaced with "East" or "West," depending on whether they fall east or west of State Street; "North" and "South" denote whether streets fall north or south of Madison Street. Address numbers increase or decrease depending on their distance in miles from the epicenter, with odd numbers sticking to the south and east sides of streets, and even numbers on the north and west sides.

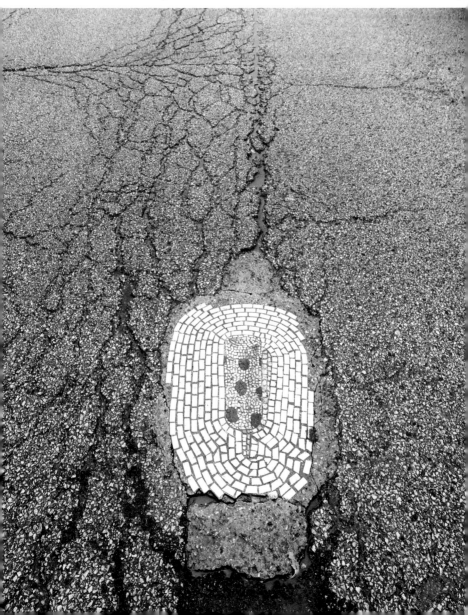

78 Pumping Station: One

Chicago's oldest and largest hackerspace

Founded in 2009, Pumping Station: One, or PS:One, is Chicago's oldest and largest hackerspace. A hackerspace is a community-operated workspace where people with common interests, such as technology, science, digital art, or electronic art, can meet, socialize, and collaborate. (The hackerspace movement launched in Germany when c-base, one of the most influential hackerspaces in the world, opened its doors in Berlin in 1995.)

Located in Avondale, PS:One spans over 11,000 square feet and is home to a vibrant community of over 500 members, including artists, engineers, software developers, machinists, woodworkers, and welders, an eclectic mix of talents and interests that fosters one of the most innovative creative spaces in the city.

This is the place to go if you'd like to play around with some of the coolest tools ever invented – plasma cutters, pressure washers, laser cutters, 3D printers, oscilloscopes, waveform generators, a blacksmithing forge, a sandblasting cabinet, a vacuum former, a powder coating oven, and more. Members can participate in workshops, classes, and events to hone skills, gain new knowledge, and connect with other creatives with big ideas through tutorials, meetups, and collaborative projects. Bonus: The space is open 24/7.

The Power Racing Series (PRS), launched here in 2009 before moving on to hackerspaces around the world, is the hackerspace's most popular annual event. PRS involves modifying and racing electric ride-on toys, like Power Wheels, all while adhering to strict rules: vehicles must be battery-powered, with a maximum of 36 volts; total build cost must not exceed $500; and vehicles must be able to go from top speed to a full stop in less than 18 feet.

If you'd like to see what it's all about, PS:One hosts weekly open house events on Tuesdays, when you can tour the space, ask questions, and learn more about the community.

Address 3519 N Elston Avenue, Chicago, IL 60618, +1 (872) 395-3874, www.pumpingstationone.org | Getting there Train to Damen (Blue Line) | Hours Unrestricted | Tip Also in Avondale, at Rockwell on the River (rockwellontheriver. com), the Chicago Electric Boat Company rents donut-shaped boats by the hour so you can take a sweet cruise down the Chicago River (3057 N Rockwell Street, www.chicagoelectricboats.com).

79 Quinn Chapel

Beacon of hope

Quinn Chapel African Methodist Episcopal (AME) Church is the oldest African-American congregation in Chicago. Established by a small prayer group of seven individuals, the congregation played a crucial role in the abolitionist movement. Its church served as a station on the Underground Railroad, providing refuge for those escaping slavery.

"This church was founded in 1847, which is 16 years before the emancipation proclamation, which is 18 years before Juneteenth is enacted," said historian and Black history advocate Ernest Crim III in an interview with CBS News. "That shows that even though we weren't a Southern state or a Confederate state, we played a role in advocating for Black folks to be free. There were Black people here who attended this church, formerly enslaved Black folks who migrated to Chicago who used their church to help Black people either gain freedom here to settle in Chicago or to help provide them with resources to move to Detroit or maybe even Canada."

When their original church building was destroyed in the Great Chicago Fire of 1871, the congregation persevered and eventually built their new, Romanesque Revival-style church in 1891. Many notable figures have stepped into this hallowed space, with its intricate woodwork and stained glass windows, designed by Charles H. McAfee, considered one of the most important Black architects and a pioneering advocate for housing equality. Frederick Douglass, W. E. B. Du Bois, Susan B. Anthony, Rev. Jesse Jackson, and Barack Obama have all stepped behind the pulpit to inspire congregants.

Dr. Martin Luther King Jr.'s speeches at Quinn Chapel were especially significant moments in the Civil Rights Movement, serving as rallying cries for action and solidarity in the fight against segregation and discrimination. Visitors are welcome to attend services in this historic, hallowed chapel.

Address 2401 S Wabash Avenue, Chicago, IL 60616, +1 (312) 791-1846, www.quinnchicago.org | Getting there Train to Cermak-McCormick Place (Green Line) | Hours Tue–Sat 9am–5pm, Sun 8am–2pm, Sunday services 10am | Tip Walk to Paul Laurence Dunbar Park and visit the monument to the African American author, poet, and playwright, who moved to Chicago in 1893 (300 E 31st Street, www.chicagoparkdistrict.com/parks-facilities/paul-laurence-dunbar-monument).

80 The Rainbo Club

Stare into the shot glass's false bottom

In Nelson Algren's 1949 classic movie *The Man with the Golden Arm*, Frankie Majcinek, a veteran of World War II, struggles to make ends meet while fighting a growing addiction to drugs and alcohol – "For way down there, in a shot glass's false bottom, everything was bound to turn out fine after all." Much of the story takes place during the immediate postwar period along Division Street and Milwaukee Avenue, Chicago's old Polish Downtown. The Rainbo Club, one of Algren's favorite local haunts, is the inspiration for the fictional Tug & Maul bar, where Majcinek tried his best to drink his cares away: "The Tug & Maul, this winter noon, looked much as it had that Easter Dawn. Frost had gathered on the windows and by night there would be neon rainbows in the snow."

Algren lived on the third floor of a three-story walkup, walking distance from the Rainbo Club at 1958 W Evergreen Avenue. Look for the plaque that commemorates his time spent in the apartment.

Dive bar par excellence, the Rainbo Club has undergone several incarnations in its long history. It has been a bar within a drugstore, a burlesque bar, a speakeasy, and a Polka-dancing watering hole, since it first opened in 1936. Despite its various transformations, not much has changed inside. It is easy to imagine burlesque dancers shimmying atop the white clam-like Art Deco stage behind the bar. Patrons still belly up to the bar or sink into the red vinyl seats, still trying their best to wash down their worries with shots, much like Frankie Majcinek in the movie and Nelson Algren, who was a regular, did in the forties. Liz Phair's 1993 album *Exile in Guyville* was inspired by the Rainbo Club, with its regular patrons who, despite the passage of time, have always fitted the down-and-out artist bill, and the neighborhood that grew up around it; the album's cover photo was shot in the bar's photo booth.

Address 1150 N Damen Avenue, Chicago, IL 60622, +1 (773) 489-5999 | Getting there Train to Division (Blue Line) | Hours Daily 4pm–2am (Sat open until 3am) | Tip At the center of Chicago's "Polish Triangle," a triangular intersection of Ashland Avenue, Milwaukee Avenue, and Division Street, lies a black cast-iron fountain, dedicated to Nelson Algren in 1998. The inscription on the fountain's base, "For the masses who do the city's labor also keep the city's heart," is from Algren's 1951 essay "Chicago: City on the Make."

81 Rebuilding Exchange
Reimagine and reuse

The Rebuilding Exchange is not just a store – it's one of Chicago's most sustainably minded spaces and a unique nonprofit organization where creativity, community, sustainability, and social impact intersect.

Rebuilding Exchange is dedicated to promoting sustainability through the reuse of building materials. This innovative space offers a treasure trove of reclaimed materials, from vintage doors and windows to unique architectural elements, all waiting to be repurposed, and all pulled from Chicago buildings destined to be torn down. In the current era of cheap construction and cookie-cutter design, older architectural materials offer a distinct charm and history that new materials simply can't replicate. They were typically crafted with higher-quality materials and techniques that are hard to find today.

Hands-on workshops here cater to all skill levels and help anyone looking to up their DIY skills. Woodworking 101 will teach you the basics of the trade, including how to use hand and power tools safely as you create simple projects. Creative Reuse workshops focus on transforming materials once destined for the trash heap into useful home items, like planters and cutting boards. In the DIY Upholstery classes, you'll learn how to breathe new life into a piece of furniture that went into the landfill. Home Improvement classes include Basic Plumbing, so you can fix your own leaks and unclog your own drains, and ultimately tackle plumbing repairs in your own home. If you have a project in mind, Rebuilding Exchange also offers open shop memberships, which allow you to use their tools and space for your own projects.

Rebuilding Exchange not only reduces waste but also supports individuals seeking careers in the building trades by offering paid pre-apprenticeship programs that provide a pathway to well-paying union apprenticeships in the building trades.

Address 1740 W Webster Avenue, Chicago, IL 60614, +1 (773) 252-2234, www.rebuildingexchange.org, info@rebuildingexchange.org | **Getting there** CTA bus 9 to Ashland & Webster | **Hours** Daily 10am–6pm | **Tip** Steps away from Rebuilding Exchange, Pagoda Red (1740 W Webster Avenue, www.pagodared.com) specializes in rare and unusual Chinese antique furniture and artifacts.

82 Robinson Woods

Where the ghosts are

Mysterious shadows, strange sounds, glowing orbs, and even an ectoplasmic mist have all allegedly been caught red-handed on camera in the ancient Native American burial ground hidden in the woods just off bustling Lawrence Avenue. If you are looking to scare your pants off at perhaps Chicago's most paranormal place, grab a flashlight and hike into Robinson Woods in the dead of night … if you dare.

Chee-Chee-Pin-Quay, a.k.a. Alexander Robinson, was the fur-dealing son of a Scottish trader and a Chippewa woman. When Fort Dearborn was attacked by the Potawatomi in August 1812, Robinson helped broker the release of the fort's captain and some of the early Chicago settlers who had been held captive after the battle. About half of today's 265-acre Robinson Wood was gifted to Robinson in gratitude. His descendants continued to live in a home that once stood here until 1955, when it burned to the ground. A large granite memorial marks the burial site of both Robinson and his French wife Catherine Chevalier, as well as many of their 14 children and grandchildren. When the city of Chicago annexed the land during construction of O'Hare Airport, city officials promised Robinson's sole living descendant that he too could be buried here among his ancestors. When he died, however, the city broke its promise, which, according to legend, set off the paranormal activity that carries on to this day.

Visitors often report hearing the sound of beating tribal drums, and smelling freshly-cut flowers even when the woods are covered with snow. Follow the unmarked footpath from the small parking lot, as it leads to some old fencing and a lane, marking the site of the Robinson homestead. Most paranormal activity seems to come from the left side of the Robinson Family Monument. In addition to ghosts, the riverside preserve is also home to deer, beavers, turtles, and mallards.

Address W Lawrence Avenue at the Des Plaines River, www.fpdcc.com/robinson-woods | Getting there Train to Rosemont (Blue Line), then Pace bus 301, 303, 308, or 332 to River & Lawrence | Hours Daily dawn – dusk | Tip For the main entrance to Robinson Woods, turn east/left on Lawrence Avenue; the parking area is on the south side of the street. To access the Robinson family burial grounds, continue east on Lawrence and turn north/left on E River Road. The small pull out is on the west side of the road.

83 Royal Palms Shuffleboard
Keep calm and shuffle on

Lighthearted, social, and fun, shuffleboard is the only sport where sliding into the DMs is encouraged. The game dates back to 15th-century England, where it was originally known as "shovelboard" and played in the courts of King Henry VIII before gaining popularity among European nobility. Though it's not an Olympic sport, shuffleboard's cousin, curling, often referred to as "shuffleboard on ice," has been part of the Winter Olympic Games since the inaugural event in 1924.

Modeled after classic shuffleboard clubs in Florida, Royal Palms Shuffleboard features ten regulation-sized courts, where guests can enjoy the game with properly tropical cocktails, flamingo-flocked bathrooms, and a delightful blend of nostalgia and modern fun. The rooftop, known as The Lido Deck, with its bar, shuffleboard court, and tropical oasis vibe, will transport you straight to vacation mode. A different food truck parks inside a special onsite garage each day, so you can order a la carte and enjoy a new style of cuisine every visit, while the full-service bar serves up coladas, daiquiris, margaritas, and more.

To join in on the shuffleboard fun, simply swing into this balmy oasis and sign up for a walk-in court. You'll receive a buzzer: Wait for a buzz, then pick up your 'biscuit caddy' – shuffleboard slang for 'disc holder' – and get your game on.

Shuffleboard courts are marked with scoring zones, including values like 10, 8, and 7, and a "10-off" zone that deducts points. Players take turns using their 'cues' to slide their discs (pucks) down the court, aiming to land them within the scoring zones without touching the borderlines. The objective is to score the highest points by strategically placing discs while knocking opponents' discs out of scoring zones. Shuffleboard can be played in singles or doubles, making it a versatile and strategic game enjoyed by people of all ages.

Address 1750 N Milwaukee Avenue, Chicago, IL 60647, +1 (773) 486-8682, www.royalpalmschicago.com, info@RoyalPalmsChicago.com | Getting there Train to Damen (Blue Line) | Hours Mon–Thu 5–11pm, Fri 5pm–1am, Sat noon–1am, Sun noon–8pm | Tip Interested in learning how to curl? Check out the Chicago Curling Club in Northbrook, where four sheets of ice welcome beginners in the "Learn to Curl" series (555 Dundee Road, Northbrook, www.chicagocurlingclub.org).

84 School of Shoemaking
Finding the sole of the city

In a former factory loft lined with exposed brick and wooden beams, a cobbler with over 40 years of experience carefully hand stitches an insole. The rich, warm smell of smooth leather permeates the air. Steel cutters, iron pliers, brass-handle awls, scissors, punches, and hammers hang from the walls and wait patiently on large wood work tables. It is a scene straight out of "The Elves and the Shoemaker." But this busy cobbler is no little old man: she's Sara McIntosh, founder of the Chicago School of Shoemaking & Leather Arts. And her elves-in-training are men and women from across the city, all eager to discover the long-lost craft of handmade shoes.

Chicago School of Shoemaking & Leather Arts is one of the few remaining schools in the world that teaches the art of shoemaking. Take one class at this school, and you'll leave with a truly unique pair of sandals, moccasins, or boots that are comfortable, sustainable, and promise to last for years. Small class sizes – no more than four students per class – and personalized instruction mean that budding cobblers will learn everything they need to craft high-quality shoes within the session timeframe, approximately 18 hours of class time. The school provides the patterns, midsoles, and soles based on your shoe size. You'll cut out the leather, prepare the materials, and stitch the leather uppers to the midsoles, glue those to the soles and then form the upper to the shape and size of your feet. After a few finishing details, you will proudly walk away in a pair of one-of-a-kind kicks.

"Our goal is to empower all people to enjoy a satisfying and liberating experience around creating footwear and leather work," declares the literature for this old-school school. "Buy a pair of shoes and you cover your feet for a year or two. Learn how to make shoes, and you can shoe yourself, family and friends for a lifetime." Whether you're cobbling for fun or for a lifetime, you'll walk away with new skills and a unique pair of shoes to boot.

Address 3717 N Ravenswood Avenue, Chicago, IL 60613, +1 (773) 334-2248, www.chicagoschoolofshoemaking.com | Getting there Train to Addison (Brown and Purple Line) | Hours See website for class schedule | Tip Learn the art of soapmaking by taking a class at the charming Abbey Brown Soap Artisan shop (1162 West Grand Avenue, www.abbeybrown.com).

85 Secret Mobster Vault
Home of the henchman

As one of Al Capone's top henchmen, Frank "The Enforcer" Nitti was in charge of the mob's "muscle" operations. He ran Al Capone's liquor smuggling and distribution operation, importing whisky from Canada and selling it through a network of speakeasies. He was one of Capone's most trusted bodyguards, and when Capone was arrested in 1929, he named Nitti as a member of a triumvirate that ran the mob during his stint in Philadelphia's Eastern State Penitentiary. Under Nitti's direction, the Chicago Outfit branched out from prostitution and gambling to control of labor unions and business extortion.

Nitti maintained a hideout at 33 W Kinzie Street, the Dutch Renaissance Revival-style former headquarters of the Chicago Varnish Company, built in 1895 and designed by Henry Ives Cobb. Under the guise of a cheese company, Nitti kept an apartment on the fourth floor from early 1939 until his death. From his window here, he could keep an eye on the nearby courthouse building; the basement was connected to the city's tunnel network, which allowed him to make a quick, covert escape.

In 1943, Nitti and other members of the Outfit were indicted for extorting the Hollywood film industry. Dreading the thought of incarceration – Nitti was claustrophobic – he sent his wife off to Our Lady of Sorrows church to pray for him. He began drinking heavily, loaded a .32 caliber revolver, walked to a local railroad yard, and shot himself in the head.

Today Harry Caray's Steak House occupies the building, but you can still sneak into Nitti's vault, which contains a remarkable collection of memorabilia, including a phonebook containing contact information for several reputed Chicago gangsters from the thirties and forties, a three-door safe from the early 1900s, and numerous original newspaper articles and photographs documenting the exploits of Nitti and his gang during the Capone era.

Address Harry Caray's, 33 W Kinzie Street, Chicago, IL 60654, +1 (312) 828-0962, www.harrycarays.com | Getting there Train to Grand (Red Line) | Hours Sun–Thu 11:30am–10pm, Fri & Sat 11:30am–11pm | Tip The Vault, accessible through Harry's Bar, can be viewed by guests at no cost during regular restaurant hours. Be sure to check out the other memorabilia showcasing the history of the Cubs and famed sportscaster Harry Caray's legacy (including a pair of Caray's iconic, oversized glasses) located throughout the restaurant and bar.

86 Showmen's Rest

Where the circus comes to rest

In the wee hours of June 22, 1918, engineer Alonzo Sargent's locomotive was pulling 20 empty Pullman cars when he fell asleep at the controls, ramming his Michigan Central Railroad troop train into a slower circus train, packed with performers, on the same tracks. Eighty-six circus members died from the impact, while another 127 were injured, when Sargent's train plowed into the caboose and four rear wooden sleeping cars of the circus train. Five days after the wreck, the many clowns, acrobats, aerialists, stuntmen, and strongmen were laid to rest in a mass grave that was dug out of a 750-plot section of Woodlawn Cemetery, that had coincidentally been recently purchased by the Showmen's League of America.

The headstones here bring the train tragedy to life. Some are inscribed with showbiz names – Baldy, Smiley; others indicate the deceased's role in the circus, such as "horse driver"; others are marked "Unidentified Male" or "Unidentified Female" – indicative of both the horrific collision and the circus lifestyle that often picked up new troupe members along the tracks to the next performance. The more famous showstoppers buried here include trapeze artist Jennie Ward Todd of the Flying Wards; strongmen Arthur Dieckx and Max Nietzborn of Great Dieckx Brothers fame; and the McDhu Sisters, noted aerialists and elephant wranglers. Five granite elephants, their trunks lowered in tribute, were added in the years that followed the tragedy, leading to rumors of ghostly circus animals wandering the graveyard at night, but the elephants that did die in the train crash were too heavy to move, and were buried beside the tracks.

Sargent was charged with manslaughter for falling asleep on the job, and the accident led to regulations mandating sleep for tired train crews. Showmen's Rest is still used today to inter deceased circus performers.

Address 7750 W Cermak Road, Forest Park, IL 60130, +1 (708) 442-8500,
www.showmensleague.org/Showmens-Rest | Getting there Train to 54th/Cermak (Pink
Line), then Pace bus 322 to Cermak & Burr Oak | Hours Daily 8am–6pm | Tip Forest Hill
Glen Ellyn Cemetery is located on the ancestral homelands of several tribal nations. A large
boulder with the carved face of a Potawatomi man marks an ancient trailhead, and there
is also a statue on Indian Hill, a gathering place for the Potawatomi people (815 N Riford
Road, Glen Ellyn, www.foresthillgecemetery.com).

87 ___ Sky Chapel
Worshipping in the clouds

Reaching 568 feet into the air, the Sky Chapel is the world's tallest church. Aptly located in the metropolis that birthed the skyscraper, this church in the clouds is home to the congregation of the First United Methodist Church of Chicago, one of the city's earliest parishes.

An elevator whisks worshippers up directly to the chapel, which is tucked under the base of the skyscraping steeple. Sixteen stained-glass windows envelop congregants here, one of which memorializes the church's original riverside cabin. At its center, an illuminated altar depicts Jesus, carved in wood, as he weeps over Chicago and its people, who are still unaware of "the things that make for peace." It is easy to keep time here, despite the timeless ambiance: every 15 minutes digital church bells ring from speakers attached to the building. This is as close to the heavens as you'll get in Chicago.

The famed local architectural firm Holabird & Roche designed the neo-Gothic Chicago Temple building, which is constructed on a steel frame faced with limestone. The skytop chapel, once the building's bell tower, was a 1952 gift from the Walgreen family (of the eponymous drugstore chain). The space seats just 30, making it a popular site for small weddings. The chapel is both intimate and awe-inspiring, thanks to its bird's-eye view of the city from the patio.

The congregation, founded in 1831, established a church of their very own on the north bank of the Chicago River in 1834. From their first house of worship, a humble log cabin, the congregation now resides in what was the city's tallest building from the date of its completion in 1924 until 1930. The First United Methodist Church stood firm about remaining in the city, despite the fact that many churches sold pricey downtown real estate and fled to the suburbs after World War I, and it boasts a diverse and welcoming membership.

Address 77 W Washington Street, Chicago, IL 60602, +1 (312) 236-4548, www.chicagotemple.org | Getting there Train to Washington (Blue Line) or Washington/Wells (Brown, Orange, Pink, and Purple Line) | Hours Daily 7am–7pm; free guided tours Mon–Sat 2pm & Sun after each worship service | Tip Is it a pigeon? A skeleton? A hungry insect? An Afghan hound? Theories abound but no one knows for sure what exactly Picasso intended to portray with his iconic, unnamed, 50-foot-tall steel sculpture, located just across the street from the main entrance to the Sky Temple.

88 The Smoke-Filled Room

Power brokering at the Blackstone

Late into the wee hours of June 11, 1920, after a disappointing, dead-locked convention at the Chicago Coliseum, a small group of US senators gathered to arrange the nomination of Warren G. Harding as Republican candidate for president, in Room 404 of the Blackstone Hotel. When the deal was done and the door to the room opened, a United Press reporter noted that Harding had been officially chosen "in a smoke-filled room" and a new political phrase was officially coined. "Smoke-filled room" has referred to power boss brokering behind the scenes ever since.

If the Blackstone Hotel could talk, oh the stories it would tell! For decades, it was the place to see and be seen in Chicago. Everyone from Rudolph Valentino to Joan Crawford, and from Truman Capote to Tennessee Williams has strutted through the Beaux Arts lobby. Best known for hosting 12 US presidents, from Teddy Roosevelt to Jimmy Carter, the hotel was built in 1909 at a cost of $1.5 million ($26.2 million today) and named after Timothy Blackstone, a Chicago politician, railroad executive, and founding president of the Union Stock Yards. From the storied secret passageway that JFK allegedly spirited through to visit the room of Marilyn Monroe, to the ballroom where the top stars of entertainment, including Dizzy Gillespie, Jay McShann, and Johnny Griffin, once filled the air with all that jazz, 20th-century history has unfolded in this charming, elegant hotel, a true, polished Chicago gem, still flawless after all these years.

You can still check into the Smoke-Filled Room, one of the Blackstone's most inviting suites, but leave your cigars at home. With its exquisite, French-inspired décor, formal foyer, dining and powder room, the historic, once smoke-filled parlor centers on the original marble fireplace and dazzles with its awe-inspiring, panoramic views of Lake Michigan and Grant Park.

Address Renaissance Blackstone Chicago Hotel, 636 S Michigan Avenue, Chicago, IL 60605, +1 (312) 447-0955, www.blackstonerenaissance.com | Getting there Train to Harrison (Red Line) | Hours Lobby hours | Tip The Blackstone also has a connection to the Chicago mob. Al Capone was a frequent guest of the in-hotel barbershop, appreciative of the fact that the barbershop had no windows. Now converted into a one-of-a-kind meeting space, the former barbershop retains its original fountain element, and you can still spot the traces of the original barber chairs on the marble floor. You might recognize the ballroom as the setting where Robert De Niro, playing Al Capone, beats two men with a baseball bat, in the Academy Award-winning movie *The Untouchables*.

89 South Side Elevated Car
Back when commuting was an elegant affair

On May 27, 1892, a six-car train carrying 300 guests rolled down 39th Street to the Congress Parkway Terminal downtown and straight into history. The South Side Elevated Railroad was the first-ever elevated rapid transit line in Chicago. Running from downtown Chicago to Jackson Park, with branches to Englewood, Normal Park, Kenwood, and the Union Stock Yards, this was the train that once shuttled fairgoers to the World's Columbian Exposition from May 1 through October 30, 1893. Much of the route that this train once rambled down is still used today as part of the iconic Chicago L system.

Though today the train is frozen in its tracks, you can still step aboard L Car No. 1 at the Chicago History Museum, where it has been lovingly restored and now welcomes passengers going nowhere. It took two days to relocate the 42,000-pound car, which had been gathering dust at the CTA's storage facility, very carefully, and then cautiously lift it into the second floor of the museum.

CTA riders today will feel like they are entering another world altogether as they step into this posh car. Pulled by steam locomotives, with doors on both ends of the car, the interiors that once greeted the city's commuters were luxurious by today's standards, complete with fine, varnished wood, ornate gas lighting, and rattan seats. The South Side Elevated Railroad provided 24-hour service, a boon to the city that works day and night. People had previously relied on cable railroads, which required daily overnight shutdown for cable maintenance.

Short for "Elevated", the Chicago L is the second-oldest rapid transit system on the continent after Boston's, and a visit to Chicago isn't complete without a ride around the Loop on the L. Though the cars have changed over the years, stepping up and onto the Brown Line at Adams and Wabash still gives a timeless perspective of Chicago from its elevated tracks.

Address Chicago History Museum, 1601 N Clark Street, Chicago, IL 60614, +1 (312) 642-4600, www.chicagohistory.org | Getting there Train to Sedgwick (Brown and Purple Line) | Hours Mon – Sat 9:30am – 4:30pm (Tue until 7:30pm), Sun noon – 5pm | Tip Don't miss the Chicago History Museum's Sensing Chicago exhibit, which gives visitors the opportunity to ride a high-wheel bicycle, hear the Great Chicago Fire, smell the Union Stock Yards, and transform into a giant Chicago-style hot dog.

90 _ Star Farm Chicago
Cultivating Community and Sustainability

The Back of the Yards, a historic neighborhood on Chicago's south-west side, was once the heart of the city's meatpacking industry. The former Union Stock Yard, established here in 1865, covered hundreds of acres and processed an astounding 18 million animals per year at its peak. Working conditions at the stockyards were notoriously harsh, with long hours, low wages, and dangerous environments. Upton Sinclair's novel *The Jungle* famously exposed these exploitative and unsanitary conditions.

Star Farm, a postage-stamp-sized, urban farm nestled in the bustling neighborhood is transforming the legacy of the unscrupulous meatpacking industry. Through initiatives like local farmers' markets, job training, and community engagement programs, this tiny, idyllic farm in the city is fostering a resilient food system and promoting food justice. By providing fresh, healthy food options, Star Farm addresses food insecurity while also promoting sustainable, urban agriculture.

A diverse array of organic fruits and vegetables rise in the farm's rich soil: kale, collards, spinach, arugula, carrots, beets, radishes, potatoes, tomatoes, cucumbers, squash, peppers, basil, mint, and garlic. Star Farm's Community Supported Agriculture (CSA) initiative allows you to purchase shares of the farm's harvest, ensuring a steady supply of seasonal fruits and vegetables delivered directly to your door.

In addition to its focus on food production, Star Farm is dedicated to social equity and inclusion. The farm provides local jobs, vocational training, and horticultural therapy to people with disabilities and those facing employment barriers.

Experience the magic of monthly Family Wednesdays, where you can tour the farm, enjoy fresh produce giveaways, and delight in cooking demos and storytelling sessions. It's a free, family-friendly adventure on the lively little farm in the city.

Address 934 W 50th Place, Chicago, IL 60609, +1 (312) 768-9949, starfarmchicago.com |
Getting there CTA bus 47 to 75th & Halsted | Hours Mon–Sat 10am–4pm; Family
Wednesdays every fourth Wed 3–6pm | Tip The Union Stock Yard officially closed in 1971,
but its gate, designed by Burnham and Root around 1875, remains as the only structural
reminder of the neighborhood's storied meat processing history (926 W Exchange Avenue).

91 Steelworkers Park
Steel dreams

US Steel provided the framework for everything from the soaring Willis Tower to the iconic steel drawbridges and even the Picasso sculpture on Daley Plaza. Founded by J. P. Morgan and attorney Elbert H. Gary in 1901, it was once the largest steel producer in the world as well the first billion-dollar corporation. The former South Works manufacturing plant on Chicago's Southeast Side, which opened in the late 1880s and was controlled by US Steel by the turn of the century, took advantage of the fresh water and easy shipping that both the adjacent Lake Michigan and Calumet River provided. African-American migrants from the south and immigrants from around the world flooded the area, eager to work in the growing steel industry. When the plant shut down permanently in 1992, the vacant space and its crumbling remains were a sad reminder of the city's shifting economy. In 2014, Steelworkers Park rose from the ashes of the South Works and was dedicated to the many workers who provided the steel frames that made Chicago rise from the prairies to the skies.

As you wander the 16.5-acre Steelworkers Park, a slice of nature in the city, it can be hard to imagine that the South Works located on this same site for over a century once employed over 20,000 workers. Yet the park is dotted with reminders, including a series of enormous concrete ore walls, now vacant storage buildings, and even a rusting crane that marks the mouth of the Calumet River. Flowers grow where molten steel once flowed. A sweeping vista of Lake Michigan and the city skyline built by US steel provide a beautiful backdrop. Southeast Side artists Roman Villarreal and Roman DeLion created the proud statue at the park's entrance depicting a hard-hat-wearing steelworker and his family. A plaque reads "Tribute to the Past. To all the union men and women and their families who shared the steel dreams."

Address E 87th Street at Lake Michigan, Chicago, IL 60617, +1 (312) 747-6651, www.chicagoparkdistrict.com/parks | Getting there Train to 87th Street (Metra Electric Line) | Hours Daily dawn–dusk | Tip Steelworkers Park is popular with breeding prairie and scrubland birds, and local birders. Be on the lookout for rare birds such as the western kingbird, northern mockingbird, black-billed cuckoo, grasshopper sparrow, great black-backed gull, orchard oriole, and Bell's vireo during the summertime.

92 Studebaker Theater

From carriages to creativity

Once upon a time, back in 1852, five Studebaker siblings founded the Studebaker Carriage Company in South Bend, Indiana. They crafted horse-drawn carriages that made Cinderella's pumpkin ride look like a rusty jalopy. They transitioned to making slick automobiles in the early 1900s.

In the late 1800s, the Studebakers summoned architect extraordinaire Solon S. Beman to design their new headquarters. In 1887, the Studebaker Building emerged, an eight-story marvel on Michigan Avenue. Carriages were assembled on the upper floors before gliding gracefully down to the showrooms below filled with eager buyers. Studebaker soon outgrew the Michigan Avenue showroom, and they hatched plans for a shiny, new warehouse on Wabash Avenue. Out went the cars and in came artists and musicians, who graced the stage of the former auto showroom, now the Studebaker Theater, housed within the newly inaugurated Fine Arts Building and officially opened in 1898. Imagine Ethel Barrymore emoting in the 1943 production of *The Corn is Green*, or Mae West strutting her stuff as *Catherine the Great* in 1945. Yul Brynner rocked *Lute Song* in 1947. Eartha Kitt graced the stage in *The Owl and The Pussycat* in 1964. In the early 50s, NBC broadcast some of the earliest live TV shows from here.

Fast-forward to 2021, when the Studebaker Theater got a makeover, complete with fancy seats, state-of-the-art gadgets, and mood lighting. It reopened in 2022, hosting NPR's Peabody Award-winning comedy news quiz show *Wait Wait…Don't Tell Me!* and local gems like the Chicago International Puppet Theater Festival.

Though the grand, gilded theater has returned to its former glory, the Studebaker Carriage Company did not fare as well. Unable to compete with the big three automakers, and despite its iconic designs like the 1953 Starliner, the early American carriage and car manufacturer shuttered in 1966.

Address 410 S Michigan Avenue, Chicago, IL 60605, +1 (312) 753-3210, www.fineartsbuilding.com/studebaker | Getting there Train to Jackson (Blue Line) | Hours Mon–Fri 7am–10pm, Sat 7am–9pm, Sun 9am–9pm; see website for performance schedule | Tip Sir George Solti Garden in Grant Park is a tribute to the Hungarian-born conductor of the Chicago Orchestra from 1969 to 1991 (337 E Randolph Street, www.chicagoparkdistrict.com/parks-facilities/sir-georg-solti-bust).

93 Taylor Street Bocce Courts
A match made in Italy

Nestled between storefronts and apartment buildings, across from the Conte di Savoia grocery store (1438 W Taylor Street), bocce players both curse and cheer one another on in Italiano as they play a game that has its origins in ancient Rome. The stakes are high on these two public bocce courts, and anyone is welcome to take a gamble and give the game a try at any time of the day.

Taylor Street is the main drag that crosses through the beating heart of Chicago's own Little Italy. Once home to a larger, close-knit Italian-American community, the 1961 decision to build the University of Illinois and the construction of the Eisenhower Expressway and the University of Illinois at Chicago Medical District forced many of the residents to disperse throughout the city and suburbs, causing Little Italy to be greatly diminished.

Many families have returned to the area in recent years as it has rapidly gentrified, and today Chicago's Little Italy, anchored by Our Lady of Pompeii church, remains a vibrant hub of Italian-American culture, with Taylor Street at the center of the action.

Matches here begin when a randomly chosen team of two, three, or four, or even a single player, throws a jack – a smaller ball, or *pallino* – from one end of the court into a zone 16 feet in length that ends 8 feet from the far end of the standard-sized court. After the pallino is successfully thrown, teams take turns trying to get their bocce as close to it as possible. All balls must be thrown underhanded.

You'll need to bring your own set of balls to play at these off-the-radar courts. Games tend to get quite heated, so plan on cooling off with an Italian lemonade from nearby Mario's (1066 W Taylor Street). Even better, sit back on one of the benches, relax, sip your limonata and watch the games unfold on a spring afternoon, when the courts hop with the best bocce players this side of Rome.

JOSEPH PAUL DiMAGGIO
THE YANKEE CLIPPER

Address Located in the passageway across the street from 1438 W Taylor Street, Chicago, IL 60607 | **Getting there** Train to Polk (Pink Line) | **Hours** Unrestricted | **Tip** Fuel up post-match with a sub sandwich from Conte di Savoia. Bring a picnic basket, and they will pack it to the brim with Italian-style sandwiches, snacks, desserts, and a bottle of wine (1438 W Taylor Street).

94 The Tiffany Dome
Grand souvenir of the Gilded Age

Featuring over 30,000 pieces of glass in 243 sections embraced within an ornate cast-iron frame, the Chicago Cultural Center's Tiffany Dome is the largest in the world of its kind. This splendid souvenir of Chicago's magnificent Gilded Age almost magically changes color as natural light pours through its stained-glass panels.

The Tiffany Glass & Decorating Company exhibition at the 1893 World's Columbian Exposition in Chicago launched the newly formed firm onto the international stage, leading to a number of important commissions in Chicago and beyond. Installed in the center's Preston Bradley Hall in 1897, the grand dome was designed by Jacob Adolphus Holtzer, an artist who made his mark with his elegant, electrified lantern, the precursor of the Tiffany lamp, also exhibited at the World's Columbian Exposition.

The dome's Tiffany Favrile glass, cut in the shape of fish scales, colored stones, and mother of pearl elements, was all fabricated in Tiffany's New York studio by the Women's Glass Cutting Department, headed by Clara Driscoll, a gifted Tiffany artisan who until recently was largely forgotten. The signs of the zodiac circle the top. At the base, a famous quote by British Author Joseph Addison is a reminder that the Chicago Cultural Center once acted as the city's central public library: "Books are the legacies that a great genius leaves to mankind, which are delivered down from generation to generation as presents to the posterity of those who are yet unborn."

Today, the Chicago Cultural Center serves as a creative hub, show-casing the performing, visual, and literary arts. Try to visit the space on Wednesdays at 12:15pm, when the outstanding Dame Myra Hess Memorial concerts, named after the British pianist who organized some 1,700 free lunchtime concerts for Londoners during World War II, are presented free of charge under the majestic dome.

Address Chicago Cultural Center, 78 E Washington Street, Chicago, IL 60602, +1 (312) 744-6630, www.chicagoculturalcenter.org | Getting there Train to Randolph / Wabash (Brown, Orange, Green, Pink, and Purple Line) | Hours Daily 10am – 5pm | Tip The Chicago Cultural Center's Sidney R. Yates Gallery, originally the library's main reading room, is a replica of an assembly hall in the Doge's Palace, Venice. The gallery's lavish interior surfaces were also created by the Tiffany Glass & Decorating Company.

95 Tiniest Home in Chicago

A postage-stamp reminder of the Great Rebuilding

Tiny houses are one of the hottest trends in real estate these days, and Chicago is home to a home that perhaps sparked the trend. Built in 1872, this postage stamp-sized house on Menomonee Street in Old Town was a relief dwelling, constructed from a pre-fab kit for families who found themselves with nowhere to live after the Great Chicago Fire.

On October 8, 1871, a fire broke out in a barn on the southwest side and soon swept through the city. For more than 24 hours, the fire smoldered, killing 300 people, destroying 17,000 buildings, and leaving one-third of the city's population homeless.

Chicagoans were determined to rise from the ashes. On the first Sunday after the fire, the Rev. Robert Collyer spoke to his Unitarian congregation outside the ruins of his church on Dearborn Street, re-marking, "We have not lost, first, our geography. Nature called the lakes, the forests, the prairies together in convention long before we were born, and they decided that on this spot a great city would be built."

Relief shanties like this 850-square-foot home were built by the thousands for homeless Chicagoans. The prefabricated tiny home kit cost just $125 and came with furnishings.

And so the city's so-called "Great Rebuilding" began with tiny homes like this charming abode. As displaced Chicagoans returned to live in the city in tiny homes like this one, they set out to create a new, urban center with innovative buildings, and a new style of archi-tecture was born: The Chicago School. This style, also known as the Commercial Style or American Renaissance Style, is characterized by the development and mastery of steel-frame construction, which led to the creation of the modern skyscraper.

Chicago's tiniest home is privately owned. Though miniscule in size, this home marks a shift in the building practices that helped lay the foundation for our iconic skyline.

Address 216 W Menomonee Street, Chicago, IL 60614 | **Getting there** Train to Sedgwick (Brown or Purple Line) | **Hours** Unrestricted from the outside only | **Tip** At the Chicago History Museum (1601 N Clark Street, www.chicagohistory.org), you can see a reproduction of a cyclorama painting depicting the breadth of the fire's path across the city. The original was a main attraction during the 1893 World's Fair. Standing nearly 50 feet high and 400 feet long, it occupied its own building on Michigan Avenue for spectators to observe.

96 Trephined Skull Exhibit

Appreciation for modern medicine

For anyone looking to have chills sent up their spine, the International Museum of Surgical Science delivers. The exhibits here deal with various aspects of Eastern and Western medicine. How were procedures, some that are easily carried out today – circumcision, bone repair, enemas, elephantiasis of the prostate reduction – conducted in the past? Founded by Dr. Max Thorek in 1954, this small but fascinating and somewhat ghastly museum will have you cringing in imaginary pain while simultaneously thanking God for modern medical advances.

The exhibits are displayed by theme or surgical discipline, with a focus on ailments once difficult to manage but easily treated today. Of striking interest is the trephined skull exhibit, located at the top of the stairs on the fourth floor. These timeworn skulls painfully illustrate trepanation, the archaic, misguided practice of drilling a hole into the skull to expose the dura mater, and thus relieve migraines, epilepsy, mental disorders, and other ailments, or to remove bone fragments from a head injury, while also assuring the release of any bad spirits dwelling within the body, and ending unusual behaviors in their unwitting host. Whether or not the people that once claimed these skulls as their own survived their trepanation is unknown, but ancient skulls show a reasonable level of healing.

Other items of note on display include an ancient Roman era enema syringe, an intact iron lung, an 18th-century self-propelled wheelchair, a Civil War-era bone saw, a turn-of-the-century hemorrhoid removal kit, kidney stones found in Egyptian mummies from the 28th Dynasty, and ancient Egyptian tablets depicting circumcision.

The museum itself is housed in a 1917 mansion designed as a Chicago-style interpretation of the Petit Trianon of Versailles. Ask the front desk attendant to show you the original, gilded elevator.

Address International Museum of Surgical Science, 1524 N Lake Shore Drive, Chicago, IL 60610, +1 (312) 642-6502, www.imss.org | Getting there Train to Sedgwick (Brown and Purple Line) | Hours Mon–Fri 9:30am–5pm, Sat & Sun 10am–5pm | Tip Head to the reconstructed turn-of-the-century apothecary and see if you can spot the various bottles of Lydia E. Pinkham's tonic remedies: these once wildly popular, fanciful potions, which promised to alleviate "female complaints," contained herbals but also a helpful percentage of alcohol.

97 Tribune Tower Façade

Fragments of history

In 1922, the Chicago Tribune newspaper hosted a high-stakes, international design competition for its new headquarters, offering a whopping $100,000 in prize money to the winning architect. Two hundred and sixty entries poured in from around the world. The winning design, drafted by New York architects John Mead Howells and Raymond Hood, called for a neo-Gothic skyscraper complete with gargoyles, buttresses, and a crown inspired by Rouen Cathedral in Normandy, France. The stunning cathedral of journalism soared to a height of 462 feet into the sky by the time it was completed in 1925, launching the Tribune as a large, important, and international newspaper housed in "the most beautiful office building in the world," the goal of owner and publisher Colonel McCormick. Reflecting this ambition is the fascinating and distinctive façade, which is encrusted with 150 fragments from historically important sites around the world.

Who gathered all the significant fragments from the four corners of the Earth? The tradition began in 1914 when McCormick himself was on assignment in Ypres, Belgium. He took time out from covering WWI and toured a medieval cathedral that had been damaged by German shelling. He pocketed a piece of the building and carried it home to Chicago. The Tribune's other foreign correspondents followed suit, bringing back rocks and bricks from their journeys. The various fragments were incorporated into the façade, giving visitors the chance to touch history, literally. All the major sites in the world are represented, from the Great Pyramid to the Great Wall, from Notre Dame de Paris to the Palace of Westminster. The tradition continues to this day. More recent embedded artifacts added to the collection include a sample from the Sydney Opera House, and a steel remnant of the World Trade Center towers destroyed during the September 11, 2001 terrorist attacks.

ANCIENT
TEMPLE
HONAN
PROVINCE
CHINA

Address 435 N Michigan Avenue, Chicago, IL 60611 | Getting there Train to Grand
(Red Line) | Hours Unrestricted | Tip One artifact was considered too precious to place on
the building's exterior façade: a fragment of the Cave of the Nativity in Bethlehem appears
on an interior wall inside the lobby.

98 Tuberculosis Sanitarium
A breath of fresh air

North Park Nature Village, with its loop leading through wetlands and open prairies populated with deer, is a wonderful place to catch a breath of fresh air in the city. Most of the people happily hiking its trails don't realize that once upon a time, the 46-acre nature preserve served as a lifesaving facility for up to a thousand patients suffering from a deadly disease.

Tuberculosis was a leading cause of death within the city of Chicago at the turn of the 20th century. The urban poor were hit especially hard. Widespread concern led to the passage of the Glackin Tuberculosis Law in 1909, and a special property tax was dedicated to treatment and control. In 1915, the city built the Chicago Municipal Tuberculosis Sanitarium, the largest municipal sanitarium in the country, a 650-bed, 32-building facility that provided short- and long-term care and treatment at no cost to unfortunate city residents suffering from often fatal TB.

The many windows, and walkways surrounding the building, demonstrate the theory that fresh air was vital for treating TB. Female patients lived in the brick cottages at the south section of today's village; the north section was reserved for men. A research facility was housed in the current Peterson Park Fieldhouse; the nature village's main lodge served as the dispensary. Today senior citizens occupy the former cottages, and only small clues indicate the sad history of this corner of Chicago: the graphic symbol of human lungs with a medical cross appears on several façades.

Mortality rates from tuberculosis declined slowly in Chicago in the early 20th century thanks to new drug therapies that controlled the disease effectively. The city planned to turn the waning hospital into a shopping center and apartments; thankfully, the neighborhood organized to transform the property into the peaceful nature oasis that it is today.

Address North Park Village Nature Center, 5801 N Pulaski Road, Chicago, IL 60646, +1 (312) 744-5472, www.chicagoparkdistrict.com | Getting there Train to Irving Park (Blue Line), then CTA bus 53 to Pulaski & Ardmore | Hours Daily 10am–4pm | Tip The annual Maple Syrup Festival, hosted every March at the North Park Nature Village, taps into trees planted for the sanitarium over a century ago, and features storytelling, crafts, and a demonstration of the maple-syrup-making process via bonfire.

99_Turtle Racing at Big Joe's

May the reptilian odds be ever in your favor

The betting is always exciting at Big Joe's "tracks." Every Friday evening at 9pm, this Lincoln Square dive bar plays host to one of the most unique, high-jinx races in the city. Six turtles compete against one another in a raucous, reptilian race to the finish. Which is the fastest turtle in town? When the turtles hit the tracks here, it is guaranteed to be an extremely slow "dash" to the finish line.

Here is how it works. Arrive early and drink lots of beer. Pitchers here run at just $8. With each pitcher of beer, you will receive raffle tickets for a chance to become an official turtle jockey. An emcee will announce the winning numbers for six turtle races throughout the night plus a special grand finale race, so don't give up, and keep drinking up to increase your turtle odds. If your number is called, you get to pick your lucky turtle from the crew of feisty competitors and head to the racing arena.

The starting point of these particular races is the center of a pool table: the turtles line up, with a cake lid covering them to prevent any false advances. Once the cake lid is lifted, the turtles race at top turtle speeds to the finish line, which is actually the edge of the pool table. Your job as jockey is to cheer your turtle on with all your might. Just don't expect this race to be a quick one.

The turtles here live their lives in the lap of luxury. Well cared for in their deluxe habitat, they are also indulged with love by both the staff and bar regulars. Spend more than one Friday night cheering them on, and you will get to know their unique names and personalities – and athletic prowess. The best part of these slow-as-molasses races is that even losers are winners. If your turtle makes it to the finish line first, you'll win a T-shirt. If you're turtle is the last one to make a move, or never makes a move at all, you'll win a free drink on the house.

Address 1818 W Foster Avenue, Chicago, IL 60640, +1 (773) 784-8755 | Getting there Train to Damen (Brown and Purple Line) | **Hours** Sun – Fri 1pm – 2am, Sat noon – 3am | **Tip** Chicagoans love a good bar competition. Streeterville Social (455 N Park Drive), a swanky rooftop bar in the Lowes Chicago Hotel, hosts life-sized Jenga competitions in the summertime. And all bets are on at Sluggers World Class Sports Bar (3540 N Clark Street), located a stone's throw from Wrigley Field, where batting cages greet baseball and beer loving patrons.

100 Tutore Cooking School

Bring the flavors of Italy to your home kitchen

From the rich, hearty dishes of the northern Alps to the fresh, seafood-centric meals of the coastal South, each region of Italy boasts its own culinary specialties.

You can learn to cook Italian cuisine and bring these authentic flavors into your own kitchen, creating meals that are both delicious and meaningful. It's not just about the food; it's about embracing a tradition of using fresh, healthy, local ingredients and enjoying meals you create with loved ones.

Sophisticated yet approachable, Tutore Italian Cooking School in Avondale specializes in teaching its students how to cook Italian regional cuisines. Founded by chefs Dean Zanella and James De Marte, who collectively bring over 75 years of experience in the fine dining industry, Tutore prides itself on teaching home chefs how to prepare regional Italian dishes rarely seen on most menus, making it a unique destination for both beginners and seasoned cooks looking to bring the best of *il bel paese* onto their home tables.

Classes range from basic techniques, like preparing gnocchi, pasta, and risotto, to more elaborate affairs, such as the "Sundays at Nonna's" class, during which you will learn how to make all the beloved, traditional dishes the way an Italian grandmother would, including Sunday gravy, braciola, and focaccia.

The cozy setting brings food lovers together. You'll all gather around the table with other Italian cuisine aficionados and sip Italian wines as you practice crafting traditional shapes, like orecchiette, farfalle, and pappardelle; master the technique of creating a creamy, perfectly cooked risotto, balancing flavors and textures; and learn to prepare classic Italian sauces from scratch, such as a bubbling Bolognese or Ligurian-style pesto.

You're bound to leave this school with not only a few new culinary skills but also a few new foodie friends.

Address 2755 W Belmont Avenue, Chicago, IL 60618, +1 (773) 942-6706, www.tutorecookingschool.com, hello@tutorecookingschool.com | Getting there CTA bus 77, 94 to Belmont & California | Hours Wed–Sun, see website for class schedule and registration | Tip Adjacent to Tutore Cooking School, the Beer Temple is a holy space for craft beer enthusiasts, thanks to its impressive selection of over 1,000 different brews, including a rotating lineup of around 20 draft beers (3173 N Elston Avenue, www.craftbeertemple.com).

101_ Twisted Scissors

On the cutting edge of punk-chic

When basic blonde highlights and a bob won't do, when you're look-ing for a mullet with razored layers dyed a metallic teal, a high-octane orange undercut, or a short feathered shag painted a rainbow of high-contrast pastels – when you're on the cutting edge of the punk chic aesthetic, there's one salon in town that's got you covered: Twisted Scissors.

This high-spirited, eco-conscious hair salon pioneered non-tradi-tional cuts and colors for everyone. Since its 2007 inception as a small storefront in Logan Square with just six stylist stations, a quirky wait-ing room adorned with vintage furniture and paintings by local artists, and a cooler stocked with PBR, Twisted Scissors has become a go-to for anyone eager to have their hair reflect their unique inner self, thanks to its eccentric charm and ultra-creative stylists. Sit back in their retro, pinup-girl glam salon, enjoy the music as you sip a beer or glass of wine, and let yourself be transformed in this rebellious hair haven.

Twisted Scissors embraces all hair types: curly, straight, long, short, thick, or thin.

"I always had short hair and thought it was terrible that I was charged women's prices, and that stood out to me as wrong," said salon co-owner Angela Bolos-Hartman. "We were the first to estab-lish gender-affirmative hair services. Because hair doesn't have a gender. Our eclectic client demographic – we style everyone from established punk rock singers to corporate CEOs – says it all: Every-one with hair is welcome here."

Bolos-Hartman and co-owner Amber Murphy-Huels are com-mitted to offering professional, innovative, and edgy services to their clients. They are also a partner with Green Circle Salons, an organi-zation that aims "to divert 90% of salon waste from landfills." Waste gets recycled, turned into energy or building material, composted, and many more sustainable uses.

Address 2001 N Point Street, Chicago, IL 60647, +1 (773) 227-1077, www.twistedscissorschicago.com, reception@twistedscissorschicago.com | Getting there Train to Western or California (Blue Line) | Hours Mon, Wed – Fri 10am – 7pm, Sat 10am – 6pm | Tip Post-haircut, pop into Pretty Cool Ice Cream (2353 N California Avenue, www.prettycoolicecream.com), a delightful, handmade ice cream shop featuring frozen delights in bar format–think popsicles, custard bars, and more–all pre-wrapped on sticks for a nostalgic, on-the-go treat.

102 Union Stock Yard Gate

Hog butcher for the world

In 1865, a group of railroad companies acquired a 375-acre swathe of swampy land on the South Side of Chicago, creating the Union Stock Yard & Transit Co., known more commonly as the Yards. By 1870, 2 million animals had been butchered in the meatpacking district that made Chicago "hog butcher for the world." By the start of the 20th century, 25,000 employees were passing through the entrance gate to the Yards, where they worked under miserable conditions to produce 82 percent of the meat consumed across the US. The Yards were easily accessible to all railroads serving Chicago, and the enormous stockyard was receiving over 12 million cattle and hogs by 1890. Journalist and novelist Upton Sinclair spent seven weeks working undercover here; his 1906 exposé *The Jungle* revealed the horrific sanitary and working conditions of Chicago's meatpacking industry, including dreadful tales of men falling into vats of boiling lard, diseased cattle being transformed into canned meat and rats accidentally winding up in sausages. Sinclair famously noted, "They use everything about the hog except the squeal." These graphic descriptions led in 1906 to the passage of the federal Pure Food and Drug and Meat Inspection Act, which in turn led to the development of the Food and Drug Administration. The meatpackers eventually formed unions, demanding better working conditions and fair compensation.

Designed around 1875 by John Wellborn Root of Burnham and Root, the limestone Union Stock Yard Gate was commissioned by the superintendent of the Yards, John B. Sherman. Over the arch of the gate is a bust of "Sherman," the beloved, prize-winning bull of this Stock Yard boss and co-founder.

The rugged gate is all that is left of the legendary Union Stock Yards, which closed following decades of decline, after over one billion animals had been processed, at midnight on July 30, 1971.

Address W Exchange Avenue at Peoria Street, Chicago, IL 60609 | **Getting there** Train to Halsted (Orange Line), then CTA bus 8 to Halsted & Exchange | **Hours** Unrestricted | **Tip** Directly behind the gate is a memorial statue for the 21 Chicago firefighters that lost their lives in the 1910 Chicago Union Stock Yards Fire. The names of 530 Chicago firefighters killed in the line of duty up to 2004 are engraved around the base of the memorial.

103__ Vavoom Pinups

Meet your retro self

If you've ever dreamed of traveling back in time and meeting a retro version of yourself, Vavoom Pinups is a time machine that will introduce you to your more glamorous, pinup alter ego. This full service photography studio will transform you from modern woman to vintage bombshell and then capture the moment in a sassy, sexy photoshoot.

When owner Heather Stumpf was about 10, sitting at her grandfather's drafting table, she came across some old pinup illustrations printed on cards in one of his drawers. Fascinated by the bombshells' beautiful curves coupled with wide red-lipped smiles on their faces, little did she know that her life's passion had just been born. "I'm a firm believer that we are all beautiful as women," declares Stumpf. "Each one of us deserves to feel iconic, timeless, and glamorous. Empowerment starts from within, but when you add the Vavoom experience, it explodes!"

When you arrive at the studio you'll trade your 21st-century duds for a sexy, silk robe. Vavoom's team of hair and make-up stylists will bring out your retro best. Then choose a new outfit, shoes and accessories from the endless closet of vintage finery. Then choose your background from a complete 1950s mint green and yellow kitchen set, a mod carpeted living room set, or even a tiki bar.

"Our clients are physically and emotionally empowered through each part of the process. Most of us haven't seen a photo of ourselves from head to toe … and when you do it's exciting, and for many women the experience is eye-opening," gushes Stumpf. "So many of our clients come back and tell us how Vavoom 'changed them' how the experience 'took them to the next level' in their own lives. Women who, after their shoot, could finally find their voice, who took that trip they always wanted, or were just ready for the next challenge. If that isn't empowering … I don't know what is!"

Address 1539 N Damen Avenue, Chicago, IL 60622, +1 (773) 726-1109, www.vavoompinups.com | Getting there Train to Grand (Blue Line) | Hours By appointment | Tip The stylists at Tigerlilie Hair Salon are specialists in the long-lost art of real vintage hairdressing. From pixies to beehives, they can make your retro hair dreams reality (4539 N Western Avenue, www.tigerlilie.com).

104 Walt Disney's Birthplace

Where the magic was born

In 1891, a young couple, Elias Disney and his wife, Flora, moved from Kissimmee, Florida to Chicago. Elias was a carpenter by trade, and he was able to secure a job at the World's Columbian Exposition of 1893. The couple purchased an empty lot at 2156 N Tripp Avenue, in Chicago's Hermosa neighborhood, for $700. Flora designed the home of her dreams, and, with his own two hands, Elias built the rectangular, frame home where they would add two more children to their family of four. Walter "Walt" Disney was born in the second-floor bedroom.

Younger sister Ruth followed suit two years later, completing the Disney family of seven. When Walt was just four, the family moved to a farm in Marceline, Missouri, the small town that inspired the Main Street USA at Walt Disney World.

Few people realize that this modest home was the birthplace of an American cultural icon, and for years it stood sadly in a state of disrepair. There are not any historical markers to indicate that this house was the birthplace of the Disney dream. It wasn't until the current owners, Brent Young and Dina Benadon, stepped in to save the day that the home began to breathe with new life. The duo purchased the property and has plans slowly to restore the home back to its early 20th-century glory. They also plan eventually to transform it into a multimedia-rich museum, as well as a center for early childhood creativity.

The Disney family returned to Chicago from Kansas City and settled on the Near West Side in 1917, after Elias Disney invested in the O-Zell Company, a jelly and juice producer. Young Walt attended McKinley High School and took evening cartooning classes at the Chicago Academy of Fine Arts. Walt Disney lived in Chicago until he became an ambulance driver for the Red Cross in September 1918, after which he was shipped to France, never to live in Chicago again.

Address 2156 N Tripp Avenue, Chicago, IL 60639, www.thewaltdisneybirthplace.org |
Getting there Train to Healy (Metra Milwaukee District / North Line) | Hours See website
for tour schedule | Tip Elias Disney not only built the St. Paul Congregational Church
(known as Iglesia Evangelica Bautista Betania today), that stands at 2255 N Keeler Avenue,
one block east and one block north of Walt Disney's birthplace, but also named his son after
the church's pastor, Walter Parr. Walt Disney was also baptized there.

105 Wild Mile Chicago
World's First-Ever Floating Eco-Park

Before Chicago became the bustling metropolis it is today, its landscape was a fascinating blend of prairies, savannas, open woods, forests, rivers, and bird-filled wetlands. These natural ecosystems spanned the region for thousands of years, creating a rich mosaic of habitats. Wetlands play a crucial role in the city's natural balance, providing a safe zone for wildlife, including birds, amphibians, and aquatic plants. But as the city grew, its skyscrapers rising into the sky, the wetlands in Cook County experienced a significant decline. Their total area shrank by 40% from the historic period (1890–1910) to the modern period (1997–2017).

The Wild Mile project in Chicago, located along the North Branch Canal of the Chicago River, reflects what might have existed before the city's development. This remarkable, floating eco-park offers a unique blend of urban greenspace and wildlife habitat. Its pontoon-based, floating gardens allow for plant roots to grow through their physical framework directly into the river. These artificial habitats recreate the natural wetland ecosystem that thrived here well before Jean Baptiste Point du Sable, a Black freeman, became the first permanent, non-indigenous settler in the area when he built a house at the mouth of the Chicago River sometime around 1790.

Visitors to the Wild Mile can enjoy a variety of activities and experiences. Stroll the winding paths and learning platforms to find out about the river's ecosystem. Rent a kayak and paddle this wild mile, or see if you can spot the birds that have returned to this creative new floating habitat. Great blue herons, the river's majestic waders, can sometimes be spotted flying overhead, while black-crowned night herons are often seen feeding along the river's edge. You might even glimpse a beaver, showcasing the improved health of the Chicago River ecosystem.

Address Access at 905 W Eastman Street, Chicago, IL 60642, +1 (708) 847-7086, www.wildmile.org | Getting there Train to North/Clybourn (Red Line) | Hours Unrestricted | Tip The Shedd Aquarium takes groups kayaking along the Wild Mile in the summertime, with an emphasis on conservation. Boats are provided by Kayak Chicago (1220 W LeMoyne Avenue, www.sheddaquarium.org/programs-and-events/kayak-for-conservation).

106 Willie Dixon's Blues Garden

"Reeling and a-rocking; What a crazy sound"

You probably already know the address for this musical garden, 2120 South Michigan Avenue, memorialized by the Rolling Stones in their 1964 eponymous hit song, recorded here at the adjacent Chess Records' upstairs recording studio during their first US tour.

Founded in Chicago by brothers Phil and Leonard Chess, both Jewish immigrants from Poland, in 1950, the Chess Records label shaped the future of American music. They captured timeless hits, like Muddy Waters' *I'm Your Hoochie Coochie Man*, Chuck Berry's *Johnny B. Goode*, and Howlin' Wolf's *Smokestack Lightning*. Once hailed as the top blues label in America, Chess Records later branched out into soul, gospel, early rock and roll, jazz, and comedy. Aretha Franklin made her initial recordings here at the tender age of 14, including the soul-stirring track, *Never Grow Old*.

Willie Dixon's Blues Garden is named after Willie Dixon, a pivotal figure in the blues genre and the foundation he established, which aims to promote, preserve, and protect the Blues. Initially, Dixon was an office assistant at Chess Records, and he later became a producer, talent scout, session musician, and staff songwriter, contributing significantly to the label's signature sound. Dixon's songs have been recorded by countless musicians in many genres and by various ensembles in which he participated. A short list of his most famous compositions include *I Just Want to Make Love to You, Little Red Rooster, My Babe, Spoonful*, and *You Can't Judge a Book by the Cover*.

Bring drinks, a picnic, and lawn chairs to the Record Row Concert Series, one of the best musical events in the city. Hosted on Thursday evenings all summer long in the storied garden, Blues artists from Chicago and beyond hit the small stage for an intimate, free, musical soiree.

Address 2120 S Michigan Avenue, Chicago, IL 60616, +1 (312) 808-1286,
www.bluesheaven.com | Getting there Train to Cermak/McCormick Place (Green Line) |
Hours Studio tours by appointment only Mon–Sat noon–4pm; see website for events in
the garden | Tip Stroll five minutes from Chess to VU Rooftop, and then catch the elevator
to the 22nd floor, where swanky cocktails and sweeping views of sparkling Lake Michigan
and downtown Chicago await (133 E Cermak Road, www.vuerooftop.com).

107 — Wood Block Alleys
Horse-drawn days

In the early 19th century, as major American cities dreamed of addressing the issue of their muddy and unsanitary streets, Boston developer Samuel Nicolson came up with the idea of paving streets with wooden blocks. His innovation made its way to Chicago, where plentiful lumber from Wisconsin did indeed make wooden blocks a cheaper and less noisy street-paving alternative. The hooves of the city's working horses pounded slightly more softly on Nicolson's paved streets. By 1871, Chicago had 37 miles of wood-block-paved streets. You can still find three wood-paved alleys hidden throughout the city, true souvenirs of Old Chicago.

The finest example (and easiest to find) is the narrow alleyway, closed to traffic, that runs between State and Astor Streets, behind the grand Gold Coast mansion of the Archbishop of Chicago. In nearby Lincoln Park, a small east-west alley just south of Webster Avenue and west of Hudson Avenue also features well-worn blocks. Yet another tiny, hard-to-find dead-end alley on the south side of Roscoe Street, just west of Inner Drive, is also paved with wood. Close your eyes and imagine when horses, not cars, trotted along our city streets.

Nicolson pavement called for white oak or cedar blocks, four by five inches wide, and twelve to fifteen inches long, laid together loosely on the four-inch side over a sand foundation, with the spaces in between packed with a mixture of gravel and coal tar. Nicolson's innovation was short lived, however, since his wood blocks were both slippery and stinky. They also tended to decay due to moisture retention. Eventually, wood blocks were replaced with brick or Belgian blocks. Contrary to popular belief, wood pavement was chemically treated and did not burn easily; though it was reported that the streets were aflame when the Great Fire of 1871 leveled the city, most wooden-blocked streets survived.

Address Alley at the rear of 1555 N State Parkway; east-west alley just south of Webster
Avenue and west of Hudson Avenue; dead-end alley on the south side of Roscoe Street,
just west of the Inner Drive | **Tip** Built in 1885 at the direction of Most Reverend Patrick
A. Feehan, the first Archbishop of Chicago, the historic Archbishop's Residence at
1555 N State Parkway has housed seven archbishops. Note that the mansion has two entry
façades, one for pedestrians and the other for horse-drawn carriage arrivals, joined at a
square corner, with entrances scaled to the streets they face.

108 World's Columbian Exposition Ticket Booth

After the fair has gone

Just 22 years after the Great Chicago Fire devastated the city, a glorious, picture-perfect "White City" rose from the ashes. American architect and urban planner Daniel H. Burnham oversaw the construction of nearly 200 grand, neoclassical buildings on more than 600 acres of land. Each stuccoed building was washed in white and illuminated with modern electric lights. Throughout the fairgrounds, gas lamps glowed, their light reflecting romantically in the many canals and lagoons. The White City was a marvelous sight to see.

But the magical White City wasn't meant to last. The grand façades were made not of marble but of staff, a mixture of plaster, cement, and jute fiber that would not survive the harsh Chicago winters for long. Shortly after the fair closed, a fire destroyed many of the buildings; the rest were torn down. Only the former Palace of Fine Arts, which houses today's Museum of Science and Industry, and the building that housed delegates to World's Congresses, today's Art Institute of Chicago, survived in their original foundation. The Maine State Building was moved to Poland Spring, Maine, and the Dutch House was brought to Brookline, Massachusetts. Few people know that one small building also survived, which can still be found in Chicagoland: an authentic World's Columbian Exposition ticket booth.

Located in the side yard of the Frank Lloyd Wright-designed Hills-DeCaro House, the ticket booth is often mistaken for a garden toolshed. It has been everything from a children's playhouse to a bunny hutch. The house remains a private residence, but it is occasionally opened for special tours, and you can always sneak a peek at the booth and imagine the days when visitors to the fair excitedly paid for their tickets to the long-gone White City.

Address 313 Forest Avenue, Oak Park, IL 60302 | Getting there Train to Harlem/Lake (Green Line) | Tip St. John Cantius Church features a main altar and two side altars that reputedly originate from the fair. The historic church was dedicated in 1893, the same year that the World's Columbian Exposition took place (825 N Carpenter Street).

109__Yin Wall City
Chinatown's herbal emporium

Yin Wall City is a bulk goods store where barrels brim with traditional Chinese medicine and natural remedies. Chinese medicine focuses on holistic and preventative care, emphasizing the balance of body, mind, and spirit through natural remedies like acupuncture and herbs.

Imagine a magical garden where each plant has a special power: ginseng, a root used in Chinese medicine for 2,000+ years, is the superhero of energy, boosting your stamina and fighting fatigue like a champ. Astragalus is the immune system's best friend, warding off colds and keeping you healthy. Ginger is the tummy's favorite, soothing nausea and aiding digestion with its spicy charm. Licorice root is the sweet healer, calming sore throats and reducing inflammation. And reishi mushroom is the Zen master, reducing stress and promoting relaxation.

At Yin Wall City you'll find all of the key herbs used in Chinese medicine, and you will also find more than a few items that usually fly under the radar for everyday shoppers, including abalone shell, known as *shi jue ming*, which is used as a treatment for various eye disorders. Dried sea cucumbers are known to ease the symptoms of arthritis. *Eucommia*, an herb derived from the bark of the Chinese rubber tree, is used to treat lower back and knee pain. And *gastrodia elata*, the dried tuber of an orchid-like plant, is reported to calm the liver.

The ginseng selection here is the largest in the city, with over fifty varieties, including prized, Wisconsin-grown ginseng. The knowledgeable staff at this herbal pharmacy is always ready to assist customers in finding the right products for their needs. That said, come prepared with a translator app on your smartphone. Herbs here are sold by the ounce. You'll also find a wide variety of loose-leaf teas, including oolong, green, black, and herbal teas, such as a Jasmine tea spiked with tiny rosebuds.

Address 2347 S Wentworth Avenue, Suite A, Chicago, IL 60616, +1 (312) 808-1122, www.yinwallcity.com | Getting there Train to Cermak/Chinatown (Red Line) | Hours Daily 10:30am–6:30pm | Tip Chinatown branch of the Chicago Public Library (2100 S Wentworth Avenue, www.chipublib.org/locations/20) stands out with its unique, feng shui-inspired design and stunning views of the Chicago skyline. You'll find Chinese language materials and a mural by CJ Hungerman called *Universal Transverse Immigration Proclamation*, celebrating the neighborhood's rich history and character.

110__Zap Props

Where the film industry stores its treasures

A set design coupled with the perfect props can bring your story to life on stage, in the movies, or in your very own home. Zap Props' huge 36,000-square-foot warehouse, one of the largest in the world, holds all the whimsical objets d'art, period pieces, and oddball items that film and theater directors crave. This unique depot manufactures unique props in-house and rents out modern and antique props to create the backdrop of your dreams. The store is packed from floor to ceiling with objects that will take you back in time or back to the future: disco balls, vintage bicycles, working phonographs, prop guns, mannequins, and more. Chances are you'll recognize many of the pieces, most of which have already debuted in a movie, television or stage production.

Chicago was a hub for motion picture production long before Hollywood became the home of the stars. In the early 1900s, there were more production companies and filmmakers based in Chicago than in any other US city. Uptown-based Essanay Studios, best known today for its series of Charlie Chaplin comedies of 1915, produced multiple silent films every week. In the 1980s, a film production revival in Chicago led to such iconic blockbusters as *The Blues Brothers*, *Sixteen Candles*, *Ferris Bueller's Day Off*, *The Color of Money*, *Risky Business*, and *The Untouchables*. A 30 percent tax credit on all film production costs within the state of Illinois, established in 2009, brought filmmakers back to Chicago.

Zap Props is the go-to spot for the film industry in Chicago, and owner Bill Rawski and his team also offer in-house printing and framing, as well as a full wood and welding shop, making it easier to customize or create one-of-a-kind design elements. Rawski himself has no idea exactly how many objects are in his endless, continuously-evolving inventory, making a trip to Zap Props a true treasure-hunting experience.

Address 3611 S Loomis Place, Chicago, IL 60609, +1 (773) 376-2278, www.zapprops.com | Getting there Train to Ashland (Orange Line) | Hours Mon–Fri 10am–5pm | Tip Before Chicago's dismal winter weather sent the movie stars out west, Essanay Studios produced silent films with such stars as Colleen Moore, Gloria Swanson, and of course Charlie Chaplin. Studio co-owner G. M. Anderson starred in the very popular Broncho Billy westerns. Though the studio stopped production, you can still visit the Essanay Film Manufacturing Company building (1345 W Argyle Street).

111 Zebra Lounge
Still swinging after all these years

An outstanding night on the town always ends at the Zebra Lounge, sipping lemon drops and singing with the piano man into the wee hours. Hidden in the lobby of a vintage apartment building in the glam Gold Coast, the Zebra Lounge has been swinging with live music seven nights a week since 1929.

It wasn't until millionaire real-estate magnate and hotelier Potter Palmer moved to the area in 1882 that the Gold Coast transformed from down-and-out swamplands to one of the swankiest spots in the city. Though Palmer's 43-room castle met the wrecking ball, the area retains its posh exclusivity. While Division Street is the home to many rowdy, college-kid populated bars, the Zebra Lounge, hidden on elegant State Parkway, is where the area's more seasoned residents cap the night with one last cocktail before tucking into bed.

Look for the discreet, black-and-white Zebra Lounge sign on the bottom left corner of the Canterbury Court façade on swanky State Parkway, and enter via the foyer. The zebra motif pops up everywhere in the intimate, safari-friendly interior: zebra lamps illuminate the bar, zebra-inspired art lines the walls, black and white stripes keep the cocktail menu in check. The 45-seat room starts swaying at around 10pm, when the lounge's signature martinis and bubbling champagne have hit the spot, and the music starts inspiring new friendships and loves.

People come to the Zebra Lounge for the piano men, a rotating crew of five piano entertainers who play all the classics, with "Piano Man," and "Fly Me to the Moon" among the top requests. An electronic keyboard tops the old Kimball piano because it is easier to amplify.

The menu at this lively lounge lists solely champagne, wine, beer, and three signature martinis, including the must-try Faster Pussycat, with its premium tequila, Grand Marnier, splash of Chardonnay, and fresh lime wedged along a salted rim.

Address 1220 N State Street, Chicago, IL 60610, +1 (312) 642-5140, www.thezebralounge.net | Getting there Train to Clark / Division (Red Line) | Hours Mon – Fri 6pm – 2am, Sat 7pm – 3am, Sun 7pm – 2am | Tip Scenes from the 1986 hit movie *About Last Night*, starring Rob Lowe and Demi Moore, were shot at Mother's. The heart sign above the door lets Division Street passersby know that this bar is a place to meet a sweetheart, if only for the night (26 W Division Street).

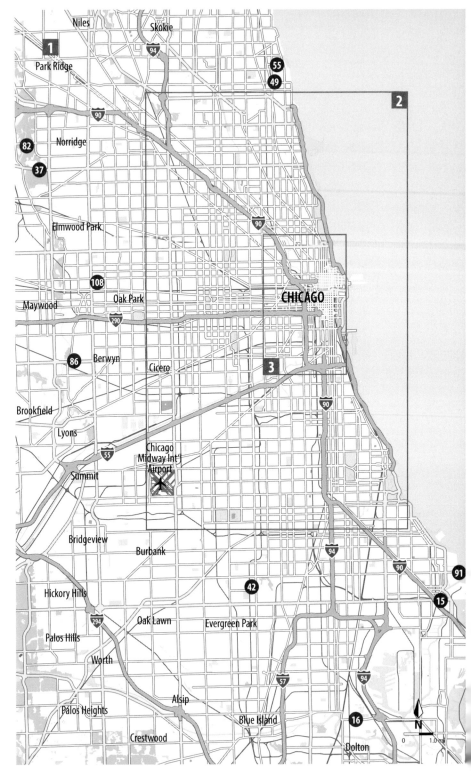

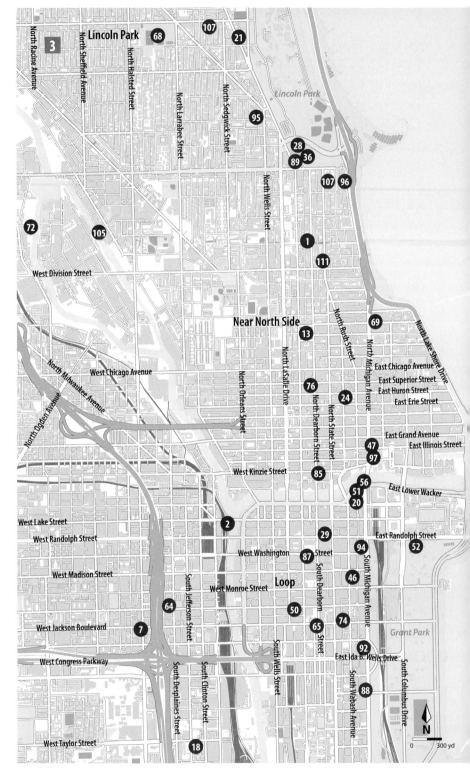

Amy Bizzarri, Susie Inverso
**111 Places for Kids in Chicago
That You Must Not Miss**
ISBN 978-3-7408-0599-9

Michelle Madden, Janet McMillan
**111 Places in Milwaukee
That You Must Not Miss**
ISBN 978-3-7408-1643-8

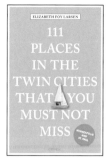

Elizabeth Foy Larsen
**111 Places in the Twin Cities
That You Must Not Miss**
ISBN 978-3-7408-1347-5

Sandra Gurvis, Mitch Geiser
**111 Places in Columbus
That You Must Not Miss**
ISBN 978-3-7408-0600-2

Brian Hayden, Jesse Pitzler
**111 Places in Buffalo
That You Must Not Miss**
ISBN 978-3-7408-2151-7

Kim Windyka, Heather Kapplow,
Alyssa Wood
**111 Places in Boston
That You Must Not Miss**
ISBN 978-3-7408-2056-5

Jo-Anne Elikann, Susan Lusk
**111 Places in New York
That You Must Not Miss**
ISBN 978-3-7408-2400-6

Evan Levy, Rachel Mazor,
Joost Heijmenberg
**111 Places for Kids in New York
That You Must Not Miss**
ISBN 978-3-7408-1993-4

Wendy Lubovich, Ed Lefkowicz
**111 Museums in New York
That You Must Not Miss**
ISBN 978-3-7408-2374-0

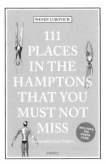

Wendy Lubovich, Jean Hodgens
**111 Places in the Hamptons
That You Must Not Miss**
ISBN 978-3-7408-2570-6

Brandon Schultz, Lucy Baber
**111 Places in Philadelphia
That You Must Not Miss**
ISBN 978-3-7408-1376-5

Allison Robicelli, John Dean
**111 Places in Baltimore
That You Must Not Miss**
ISBN 978-3-7408-2571-3

Andrea Seiger, John Dean
**111 Places in Washington
That You Must Not Miss**
ISBN 978-3-7408-2399-3

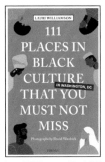

Lauri Williamson, David Wardrick
**111 Places in Black Culture
in Washington, DC That You
Must Not Miss**
ISBN 978-3-7408-2003-9

Kaitlin Calogera, Rebecca Grawl,
Cynthia Schiavetto
**111 Places in Women's History
in Washington That You Must
Not Miss**
ISBN 978-3-7408-1590-5

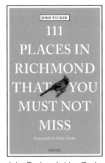

John Tucker, Ashley Tucker
**111 Places in Richmond
That You Must Not Miss**
ISBN 978-3-7408-2002-2

Cristyle Egitto, Jakob Takos
**111 Places in Palm Beach
That You Must Not Miss**
ISBN 978-3-7408-2398-6

Susan Veness,
Simon Veness, Kayla Smith
**111 Places in Orlando
That You Must Not Miss**
ISBN 978-3-7408-1900-2

Travis Swann Taylor
**111 Places in Atlanta
That You Must Not Miss**
ISBN 978-3-7408-1887-6

Dana DuTerroil,
Joni Fincham, Daniel Jackson
**111 Places in Houston
That You Must Not Miss**
ISBN 978-3-7408-2265-1

Dana DuTerroil, Joni Fincham,
Sara S. Murphy
**111 Places for Kids in Houston
That You Must Not Miss**
ISBN 978-3-7408-2267-5

Kelsey Roslin, Nic Yeager,
Jesse Pitzler
**111 Places in Austin
That You Must Not Miss**
ISBN 978-3-7408-1642-1

Philip D. Armour, Susie Inverso
**111 Places in Denver
That You Must Not Miss**
ISBN 978-3-7408-1220-1

Travis Swann Taylor
**111 Places in Phoenix
That You Must Not Miss**
ISBN 978-3-7408-2050-3

Laurel Moglen, Julia Posey,
Lyudmila Zotova
**111 Places in Los Angeles
That You Must Not Miss**
ISBN 978-3-7408-1889-0

Brian Joseph
**111 Places in Hollywood
That You Must Not Miss**
ISBN 978-3-7408-1819-7

Floriana Petersen, Steve Werney
**111 Places in San Francisco
That You Must Not Miss**
ISBN 978-3-7408-2058-9

Floriana Petersen, Steve Werney
111 Places in Napa and Sonoma That You Must Not Miss
ISBN 978-3-7408-1553-0

Floriana Petersen, Steve Werney
111 Places in Silicon Valley That You Must Not Miss
ISBN 978-3-7408-1346-8

Harriet Baskas, Cortney Kelley
111 Places in Seattle That You Must Not Miss
ISBN 978-3-7408-2375-7

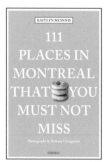

Kaitlyn McInnis, Bethany Livingstone
111 Places in Montreal That You Must Not Miss
ISBN 978-3-7408-1721-3

Jennifer Bain, Liz Beddall
111 Places in Ottawa That You Must Not Miss
ISBN 978-3-7408-1388-8

Jennifer Bain, Christian Ryan
111 Places in Calgary That You Must Not Miss
ISBN 978-3-7408-1559-2

Dave Doroghy, Graeme Menzies
111 Places in Vancouver That You Must Not Miss
ISBN 978-3-7408-2150-0

Dave Doroghy, Graeme Menzies
111 Places in Victoria That You Must Not Miss
ISBN 978-3-7408-1720-6

Dave Doroghy, Graeme Menzies
111 Places in Whistler That You Must Not Miss
ISBN 978-3-7408-1046-7

Photo Credits

© Photographs: Susie Inverso, Crimson Cat Studios, except:
3 Arts Club Courtyard (ch. 1): RH
Alfred Caldwell Lily Pool (ch. 6): S.P. Fargo
Calumet Water Retention Plant (ch. 16): Metropolitan Water
    Reclamation District of Greater Chicago
Colleen Moore Fairy Castle (ch. 26): Museum of Science and
    Industry, Chicago
Full Moon Fire Jam (ch. 38): Ryan Brandoff
Graveface Records (ch. 40): Ryan Graveface
Maggie Daley Park Skating Ribbon (ch. 52): Chicago Park
    District
Morgan Shoal and Shipwreck (ch. 60): Eric Allix Rogers
Palmisano Park (ch. 71): Robert Sit, site design group, ltd.
Poetry Foundation (ch. 76): Heinrich Blessing
Tiniest Home in Chicago (ch. 95): Ashley Black
Tutore Cooking School (ch. 100): Michael De Marte Photo

Acknowledgements

A galaxy of thanks goes to my husband, Justin, for encouraging me to do what I love, and to his family who allowed me to drag them around Chicago on a beautiful March day (one of the few!) to complete the photography of the outdoor locations.
– *Susie Inverso*

Amy Bizzarri is an extreme Chicago-history buff and freelance writer. She lives with her two children in a circa 1910 home in the Logan Square neighborhood of Chicago. When she's not writing, you'll most likely find her swimming laps at Holstein Park pool, riding her bicycle around Humboldt Park or sharing an atomic sundae at Margie's Candies with her two kids, Daniel and Chiara.

After spending many years running around Chicago photographing weddings, families, musicians, and actors, **Susie Inverso** now runs Crimson Cat Studios Pet Photography in Lakewood, Colorado. She ventures back to Chicago at least twice a year and is proud to call it her hometown.

The information in this book was accurate at the time of publication, but it can change at any time. Please confirm the details for the places you're planning to visit before you head out on your adventures.